GRAPHIC DESIGN
AND REPRODUCTION TECHNIQUES

Graphic Design and Reproduction Techniques

Peter Croy

Visual Communication Books

Hastings House, Publishers
10 East 40th Street
New York 10016

English Edition, © 1968
by Focal Press Ltd.

Translated by G. P. Burden
from GRAFIK, FORM & TECHNIK
© 1964 Musterschmidt-Verlag, Berlin

ISBN: 8038-2654-0
Library of Congress Catalog Card Number: 68-16002

First American Edition Published 1968
Hastings House, Publishers, Inc.
Second Impression 1970
Third Impression 1976

Printed and bound in Great Britain by Staples Printers Limited at
their Rochester, Kent, establishment.

CONTENTS

Contents

Contents

Contents

Contents

9

Contents

FOREWORD

This book tries to give an answer to all questions on the technical aspects and practical problems of graphic design. It is meant to be a reference work as well as a basic textbook for this field. It should help the reader to develop his own ideas, and enable him to influence them from the first designs through to the finished printed product. When you know exactly how things are printed and what possibilities are open to you, you can prevent mistakes and surprises from creeping in, and can not only demand, but recieve, the highest quality printing. You, as client, can expect conscientious work from the printer, but the printer expects clean, correct, and exact designs from you in order to produce satisfying results.

The graphic designer, especially, is often confronted with technical difficulties in the execution of a commission. Why does he not take advice from an expert, a compositor, a printer, a photographer, or a colour-analyst? The designer should in general know how to advance the work through its various stages, but to do this he must be able to communicate his ideas to those who take the job on, and must be able to oversee the project. How is the designer to keep a job under control when he is not clear about all stages of the transformation from design to printed page? The best design ideas are often dismissed because of a lack of practical knowledge; the right solution is shunned, the designer falls back on known technology and avoids experiment.

Many graphic designers will not venture to use photography as an advertising medium because of lack of experience, but photography is the ideal method of giving a truthful and realistic representation of an object or situation. The printed word is given help and support by the picture. A direct impression does not tax the imagination of the consumer unduly, and he can relate the main points of the accompanying text directly to the product. Why forego this welcome and satisfactory solution.?

13

All these questions will be answered in the following chapters. A survey is given of the work of all those people concerned, including art directors, graphic designers, commercial artists, illustrators, photographers, typographers, editors, printers, compositors, colour-analysts, draughtsmen, and many others. This book will be useful as a reference book and textbook for students in art and design schools, and for student-draughtsmen and photographers.

INTRODUCTION

Printing, the reproduction of an original by transferring ink on to paper under pressure, is the job of the printer. There are three basic types of printing processes: relief printing, planographic, and intaglio.

Relief printing is the oldest printing process known to us. In the earliest days woodcuts were used, but in 1445 Johann Gutenberg invented the single movable metal letters, which could be combined to form words and lines of type. This improvement was so great that our modern printing does not differ in basic principle.

All firms equipped for relief letterpress printing are called "printing works" regardless of their size. A small printer has at least a hand-composing room, where the single letters are set to form words and lines, assembled in a forme, inked and pressed against the paper to give an image. A larger works may have in addition one or more composing machines and machine presses. The largest works have rotary presses also for newspaper or magazine printing, and usually have facilities for making illustration blocks from photographs and drawings. Such large concerns may include planographic and intaglio departments, and a finishing shop where binding, checking, and packing is carried out.

Until recently between 70 and 80 per cent of all printing was done on the relief principle. Offset lithography is now widely used and photogravure has many applications, especially for magazine, packaging and speciality printing.

The various printing processes differ not only in method but also in their qualitative and economic characteristics. All these factors must be weighed against one another for the client and designer to decide which process is the most rational for their purpose.

Before starting a large printing job, it is advisable to relate the estimated costs to the quality attainable with each method. It is no use deciding the issue on cost alone: bad printing reduces not only the advertising impact of a work, but with it the whole value of the project.

Photography is a much later addition to the printer's armoury and it is still developing as a means of improving the presentation of printed matter. Straight-forward photography, as a method of illustrating catalogues, advertising literature, newspapers, maga-zines and innumerable other printed items, has applications too obvious to need stressing. Photo-graphic materials can, however, be used in a variety of ways to assist the graphic designer in his search for originality and impact in more specialized fields of printing.

The many techniques that can be used by the competent cameraman are detailed towards the end of this book, together with advice on the preparation of photographic artwork in a manner to get the best results in the final reproduction.

Photography in graphic design often depends on much more than straightforward camera work. So-called "trick" photography is frequently used, as is extensive afterwork in the form of retouching, air-brushing, the addition of lettering, montage, etc.

A knowledge of the processes involved is of value to all connected with graphic design, whether they actually operate the camera or commission the art-work. Photography can add a new dimension to printed matter. The imaginative use of the photo-graphic process is one of the most important aspects of graphic design.

LETTERPRESS OR RELIEF PRINTING

In letterpress printing, the raised parts of the printing forme are coated with a viscous printing ink and pressed on to the paper. Letterpress printing is used mainly for the reproduction of text, and gives the best possible quality. The letters are printed direct from the forme, whereas in planographic or intaglio printing they are photographically produced together with the illustrations on the printing plate, or cylinder.

Printing types

The letters used in composition are cast in metal—an alloy of lead, antimony and tin. A single type character consists of a body carrying a raised and laterally reversed form of the letter. Spacing material, used to fill the spaces between words, and "leads" used to fill

The elements of letterpress printing:
1 Forme (lines of type)
2 Inking
3 Laying on the paper
4 Printing
5 Removing the printed sheet

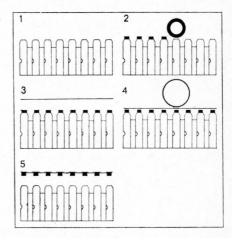

the spaces between lines in the text, is not as high as printing type, and may be softer, having more lead and less antimony. Strips of wood or plastic material ("furniture") are used to fill spaces around the pages of text in the forme.

The following terms are applied to the printing type: "the body" or "shank" is the base of the type and carries the "face", the printing surface. All English and American types have a standard "type height" or "height to paper" of 0·918 in. (23·3 mm.). The "body size" is the height of the body, and varies of course with the "type size", the size of the letter. The "set", or width of a type varies from letter to letter, M being much wider than I for instance. The shank of each piece of type has a "nick", a groove in the side which acts as a guide to the compositor in setting the type the right way up. In the "foot" or base of each type body is a groove where the tang from the mould is snapped off. This groove has nothing to do with the function of the type. Both capital and lower-case letters are printed on the base line.

All our founts (pronounced "font") of type consist

A piece of printing type representing the letter "n"

1 Body or shank
2 Face
3 Type height
4 Set or width
5 Body size
6 Nick
7 Base line
8 Groove

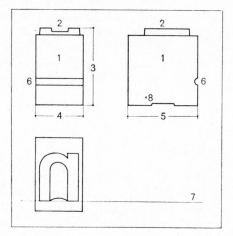

The type height and body size remain constant throughout any one fount. The set varies according to the width of the letter

The nick or nicks on the type bodies take various forms

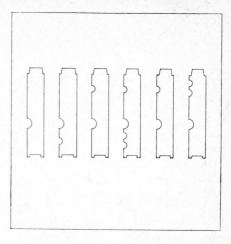

of capitals (caps.) and lower-case (l.c.) letters. The letters a, c, e, i, m, n, o, r, s, u, v, w, x, and z, are printed on the base line and their height is called the x-height. The legibility of any fount depends to a great extent on its x-height. Six letters, b, d, f, h, k, and l, have ascenders which protrude above the x-height, and five, g, j, p, q, and y, have descenders going below the base line. The capitals of most type faces are the height of the ascenders + x-height of their lower-case, but this is not always the case. To measure the size of a type, draw a pencil line just touching the tops of all ascenders, and another parallel line touching the bottom of the descenders. A type rule will now give the distance between the two lines directly in points, and this is the type size.

Type faces

Type foundries produce a large number of type faces, ranging from ancient classical types to variations of brush and pen lettering. The printer usually has sample sheets or a type specimen book showing what type faces and sizes he has in stock, and will say whether he composes by machine or by hand.

Body type is suitable for the composition of simple texts for books or magazines and is generally easy to read. Today body type is largely set by machine by either the Linotype or the Monotype system.

In the founder's type specimen sheets the abbreviations indicate for which composing machine the types are available.

We can group type families into three main classes:

I.   Round.
II.   Broken or Black Letter.
III.   Script.

Round types can be divided into three classes:

I.1   Roman types, with thick and thin strokes and serifs, or finishing strokes, at the top and bottom. Broadly speaking, roman types are split into old face and modern. Old faces have oblique stresses and serifs, whereas modern faces have vertical stresses and flat serifs. Baskerville, Bodoni, Garamond, Plantin, and Times are some of the widely used roman types.

I.2   Sans serif, with strokes of even thickness and without serifs. Some sans serif types are Gill Sans, Folio, Futura, and Univers.

I.3   Egyptian types, with even strokes and slab serifs. Clarendon, Figaro, and Rockwell are among these types.

II.   Broken letters, often called black letters, include the German Fraktur and Old English types.

III.   Script types are faces cut to resemble handwriting.

Type variations
Weights

Most type faces are delivered in different "weights", in addition to their normal weight. These are of the same basic design but are heavier, or lighter. The usual range of weights is: extra light, light, medium, bold, and ultra bold. Bold and ultra bold faces can be used to accentuate words or lines when the remaining text is set in medium weight.

Condensed and extended faces

Condensed faces are long, thin variations of the normal type. They are useful for displaying in narrow spaces. Extended or wide faces are broader variations of the normal type.

Italics

Italics are sloping roman types. Most type faces have an italic version.

Upper and lower case

The large letters of a fount are called capitals, abbreviated to caps. The small letters are called lower case (l.c.).

*	†	‡	§	‖	¶	☞	fb	ẞ	@	°/₀	ª/c	/	o
¼	½	¾	⅛	⅜	⅝	⅞	§	£	2 em	3 em	ˊ	˜	ˋ
⅓	⅔	&	Æ	Œ	æ	œ	—	-	2 em	3 em	&	Æ	Œ
A	B	C	D	E	F	G	A	B	C	D	E	F	G
H	I	K	L	M	N	O	H	I	K	L	M	N	O
P	Q	R	S	T	V	W	P	Q	R	S	T	V	W
X	Y	Z	J	U	[	(	X	Y	Z	J	U		ffl

ffi	fl	5 em	4 em	’	k		1	2	3	4	5	6	7	8
j	b	c		d	e		i		s		f	g	ff	9
?													fi	0
!	l	m	n	h		o	y	p	w	,	en qds	em qds
z												
x	v	u	t	3 em spaces	a	r	;	:	quads
q							.	-	

Above. Old style type case   Below. Modern equivalent

ffi	fl	5 em	4 em	’	k		1	2	3	4	5	6	7	8	§		Æ	Œ	æ	œ
j	b	c	d	e		i		s		f	g	ff	9	A	B	C	D	E	F	G
?										fi	0							
!	l	m	n	h	o	y	p	w	,	en quads	em quads	H	I	K	L	M	N	O
z											
x	v	u	t	3 em spaces	a	r	;	:	2 em and 3 m quads	P	Q	R	S	T	V	W
q							.	-		X	Y	Z	J	U	&	ffl

This name is a remnant of the time when two composing cases were used, the upper containing capitals, and the lower one containing small letters.

Book founts often contain a series of small capitals. These are generally about the same height as the lower-case letters.

Spacing material
Leading between lines

An 8 pt. type face on an 8 pt. body, set line upon line, fills the paper fully, but appears too heavy and is hard to read. This is called "solid matter". The appearance of the print can be altered by "leading", which is the spacing out of the lines of type by strips of lead ("leads") slightly lower than the type. A page set with the lines separated by leads is called "leaded matter".

Line-spacing material is available in many sizes

1 Short leads

2 Clumps (metal) or reglets (wood)

The composing machine can be set to cast type on various sizes of body. An 8 pt. face on a 9 pt. body is called 8 on 9 pt. Other variations, such as 9 on 10 pt., 6 on 8 pt., and so on, are possible.

Justification

The spaces between the words of a line of type are normally adjusted so that the line is filled, "justified" or set to the correct measurement. This is called "word spacing". It ensures that the lines form a neat block of type, and when evenly done can contribute to a harmonious-looking page. The pieces of metal used are called "spaces" and are lower than the type face. Sometimes a space works up in the press and prints an image on the paper, known as a "rising space".

Letter-spacing

"Letter-spacing" is done by inserting hair-spaces between the individual letters of a word. This can be used to give an optically balanced word or to emphasize a word. It is often used for a word set wholly in caps or small caps.

Rules and ornaments

For the reproduction of rules of various kinds in tabular matter, column lines, and underlining for emphasis, type-high strips of brass or typemetal in different thicknesses and patterns are used. The rules can be obtained in several lengths and it is possible to produce a wide range of variations in the composition of type area.

Ornaments or printers' flowers are specially cast type units for use as decoration. Under the same category can be found vignettes and decorative initials. Set in rows it is possible to produce decorative rules or borders.

Every printing house stocks in addition to the abovementioned a number of different signs and symbols including asterisks, mathematical and botanical signs, phonetic symbols, etc.

Kinds of type-setting

Nowadays in letterpress we differentiate between three kinds of type-setting: job-setting, text- or body-setting, and newspaper-setting. Job-setting includes such composition as can be found in headings, book-jackets, letter-heads, certificates, small-

An adjustable composing stick used for handsetting lines of type before transferring them to a galley

advertisements, etc.—in fact any work not including running texts. For this kind of setting there is a wide range of different types and type-sizes to be obtained. Job-setting is done mostly according to hand-drawn sketches and the charges are usually higher than those for body setting. Text matter is generally original "copy" or manuscript. An ample supply of the founts used must be available for hand-set corrections to the machine-set matter. News-setting is made up of body-setting and job-setting which includes small-ad-setting (ad=advertising). These are mainly done on a machine. Only the headings are set by hand and inserted to complete the forme.

Composing-machines

One differentiates between two main kinds of machine in the range of composing-machines. Line- or slug-setting such as Linotype or Intertype and single-unit-setting such as Monotype.

Linotype

This machine produces lines of type, that is to say instead of each letter being cast individually, complete lines of type emerge from the machine. The compositor taps the letters out on a keyboard. When a key is depressed a matrix bearing a female die of the chosen letter is released from a storage magazine at the top of the machine, and is carried to an assembly box. A line of matrices is produced according to the letters tapped out. Spacing is effected with a system of mechanical wedges, but if a line is too long for the measure, the

The Linotype machine sets type in complete lines. Corrections entail resetting the whole line

When the type has been set, it is transferred to a galley to await insertion into the forme

operator must decide whether to carry a word to the next line, or to split it and hyphenate.

A pump forces molten metal into the line of recessed character dies in the matrices. The machine then trims each cast line of type to type-height and body-size and further places it on a tray (named a "galley") to form running text.

On its return journey, an elevator brings the matrices to a distribution box where they are sent into their respective magazines.

For the emphasis of individual terms (accentuation) words can be set in italics or bold face on the same machine.

The various models of the Linotype system make possible almost all the kinds of setting known today. However, the system is mainly used for uncomplicated settings. One disadvantage of the system is that if a correction is necessary, the whole line has to be reset. This is not the case in the Monotype machine where the individual letters can be corrected by hand. The Intertype machine, also line-setting, works very much on the same system as the Linotype.

Monotype

Keyboarding and casting are done separately on two different machines in the Monotype system. It is preferred for scientific copy, tabular matter and difficult settings.

The keyboarding produces a punched wide paper-roll. On each edge of the paper there is a row of perforations which are gripped by spiked wheels

25

Letterpress or Relief Printing

The Monotype machine sets type in
individual characters. Corrections can be
made by hand

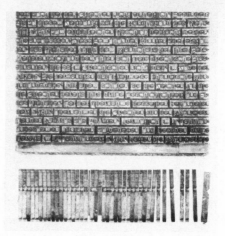

driving the roll forwards at a steady pace. When the
machine-operator taps a letter on the keyboard a hole
is made in the paper. Each character is represented
by a combination of holes punched at a varying
distance from each other. Completion of the line is
indicated by a bell.

The tapped-out roll is then inserted into the caster
machine. The matrix case is in the form of 225–255
individual letter matrices laid in rows in a rectangular
forme. Under this forme is the melting-pot with the
mould and pump. The movement of the matrix can be
controlled both horizontally and vertically.

During the moulding a jet of air is directed on to the
paper spool and the various combinations of holes determine the positioning of the matrix-case and its individual negative images. Each letter matrix is in this way
placed over the moulding pump and cast. The characters then move on to a galley in equally spaced out lines.
The compositor then binds the block of type together
with cord, to prevent"pie-ing" (falling apart) before the
block is secured in a frame in readiness for printing.

As the name indicates the galley produced on a
Monotype caster is composed of individual type and
spaces which allows great flexibility of setting and
correcting. The Monotype is very suitable for complicated setting requiring tabulations in narrow width
columns and for scientific books, etc.

Normal setting

The quality of setting is determined largely by the
evenness of the spacing of each line. Owing to the fact

that running texts in magazines and books are mostly solid settings, it is necessary to achieve even spacing, that is to say optically equal spaces between words. Corrections must be carried out by hand so that the lines are of equal length and solid. This is especially necessary for machine-printing; if the lines are badly spaced, the column of type fits together badly, resulting in the creeping up of spaces to type height so that they will print. Uniform spacing in narrow setting presents special difficulties.

Typograph

Another kind of line-setting machine is the Typograph. This machine sets and moulds lines of type but does not trim. It is economical for small printing-houses and a very reasonable investment. As in the case of Linotype, Monotype and Intertype, this machine produces lines of type with furniture and other type material. However only one type face with its accents can be produced at one time.

Ludlow

In newspaper setting, bigger type-sizes for headlines are often composed on a matrix handsetting line machine—the Ludlow. Matrices are set in lines by hand and moulded within 10 seconds on the machine. The time wasting task of re-distribution necessary in hand-composing is eliminated in the Ludlow system. As in the other systems, the blocks of type which have completed their task on the printing-machine are put back into the melting-pot. The molten metal is continually replenished with a little tin in order to retain an even consistency and to harden the metal against wear and tear during the printing.

Photo-typesetting

Photo-typesetting or filmsetting provides means to produce type matter on photographic film for making litho plates, photogravure cylinders and "wrap-round" plates for letterpress printing. It is a direct method which has become an important alternative to the various "conversion" systems for making printing surfaces from metal type.

Photo-typesetting systems may be divided into the categories of "major" ones used mainly for newspapers, magazines, directories, and book printing, while the "minor" systems have applications in commercial printing and display work. Some of the machines in the major category resemble hot-metal composing machines in their general design, with transparent matrices taking the place of metal ones, and an optical system for photographing on film in place of the casting mechanism. The matrices may be set by direct keyboard operation, or the characters, together with instructions, may be coded on paper tape on a keyboard unit; the tape is used to control one or more typesetting units. Apparatus of this kind, based on mechanical principles, continues to serve a useful purpose during the transition period from metal to film, but further possibilities are opened up by the design or apparatus based on electronic principles.

In some electronic systems perforated paper tape controls the selection of characters from a revolving disc, and they are photographed by electronic flash of such short duration that a sharp image is ensured.

High-speed electronic machines have also been developed. In a typical case the matrix carries a large number of characters (e.g. over 500). The required characters are selected by electronic switching, and they are photographed by a number of flash tubes, a line at a time. Machines in the high-speed category produce up to forty or more characters per second.

Headline and display photo-typesetting

There are numerous makes of machine of relatively simple design in the "minor" category suitable for headlines, captions, and display work. The characters are often in negative form on a strip or disc; they are selected by manual operation and optically projected on to photographic film or paper.

Computer control

The operation of "justification" to produce lines of equal width is done more or less automatically on a composing machine, but the operator has to make decisions about the splitting and hyphenation of words that would over-run a line. In addition there are many other operations requiring decisions and manual control, such as change of type (e.g. to bold or italic), corrections, provision of blank spaces for illustrations, insertion of headlines, captions, etc. Any or all of these operations are capable of automatic control with the aid of a suitably programmed computer.

Instructions for the required function may be coded on tape at the keyboard stage; the tape is fed to the input of the computer which carries out the necessary steps to produce a new tape at the output to control photo-typesetting or hot-metal composing machines.

Filmset make-up and corrections

Page make-up and the correction of filmset material involves problems of alignment which do not arise with metal type, but the technique allows of greater flexibility in positioning the work which is sometimes an advantage, especially in display composition. Page make-up is normally carried out over a ruled grid or layout sheet on a lighted mounting table. The films are cut and mounted accurately in position with the aid of a clear adhesive or transparent tape. Corrections are generally made by cutting out incorrect lines and inserting new ones. Photographic stripping techniques may be used for this work.

The corrected pages are finally "imposed" or "planned" on a transparent film base to make the complete sheet. Line or half-tone illustrations may be inserted at this stage to make the final "montage" or "flat" ready for printing-down.

Pictorial representation in print

Line drawings in black and white, continuous-tone monochrome or colour subjects are reproduced in the form of relief blocks or plates for letterpress printing. Blocks, which carry a laterally reversed image, are formed with zinc or copper plates secured to wooden or metal mounts to make them type high. The blocks are inserted in the type forme, generally along with type matter. Thin metal "wrap-round" plates of type, line and half-tone subjects are coming into use for rotary printing, as are also segmented plates made on thicker metal.

Line Blocks

Line blocks are relatively inexpensive in comparison with half-tones. Line drawings and type reproduction proofs can be reproduced by line blocks so long as no graded tones are needed, although "tints" formed with a pattern of dots or fine lines may be added to the original or introduced by the photo-engraver.

A photographic negative to the required size is first made on film or plate in a special reproduction camera.

The negative has clear lines on an opaque background. A metal plate (0·964 in. or 1·6 mm. thick, and therefore called 16-gauge metal) is cleaned and coated with a light-sensitive film. The liquid coating is spread thinly and evenly, and dried on a mechanical "whirler". The negative is put into contact with the prepared metal plate in a vacuum pressure frame and exposed to powerful arc lamps, or similar high-intensity light source. The light hardens the coating in the clear line areas under the negative so that, with suitable reinforcement, it becomes impervious to aqueous solutions.

Zinc plates are etched in an aqueous solution of nitric acid. Copper plates, which are sometimes used for fine work, are etched in ferric chloride solution. The margins and back of the plates are protected with

Enlarged detail from a line block

A print from the same block

a lacquer impervious to acid. The plates may be etched in a "rocking-bath" or in an etching machine designed to project the acid solution on to the plate. The acid dissolves bare metal, while the hardened line areas are not attacked; in this way a relief image of the original is obtained.

To prevent the acid etching the sides of the lines, it is necessary to protect them, using one of several alternative techniques. In one method the plate is rolled-up with a form of printing ink to cover the top and sides of the lines; it is reinforced with "dragon's blood" resin powder which is fused by heat treatment. The process of rolling-up, powdering, and etching is repeated in successive stages until sufficient printing depth is obtained. Large areas are afterwards routed out mechanically, and repairs and minor corrections are made by hand-engraving methods. The edges of the plate are then trimmed and bevelled, and it is mounted on wood or metal to form the finished block.

Single-step or "powderless" etching

A fairly recent innovation enables line-etching to be completed in one step in a specially designed etching machine, using a suitably formulated etching solution. The latter contains additives which make it possible to etch the bare metal and simultaneously protect the sides of the lines. The metal used is generally tough zinc or magnesium alloy having good durability for printing large editions. Segmented plates, cylinders, and wrap-round plates are made by this technique for rotary printing on sheet-fed or web-fed rotary machines

Half-tone blocks and plates

Half-tone blocks and plates reproduce gradation of tone between black and white; for this reason a reproduction of a full-tone photograph, wash-drawing or painting can be included with type in the printing forme, or etched along with type-matter to make a relief plate for rotary printing.

When a half-tone print is examined under a magnifying glass it will be seen that the picture consists of numerous small dots of various sizes. In the light areas, the dots are tiny specks; they are larger in darker areas, and continue to grow until they form a near solid in the shadow areas.

The dots are formed with the aid of a half-tone screen in the reproduction camera. The normal half-tone

31

Letterpress or Relief Printing

An enlarged section of a zinc halftone block. The round depressions are the spaces between the dots. They leave no impression, so the top, left-hand part will print darker than the bottom, right-hand part

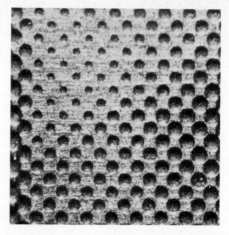

screen is formed with two glass plates, in which ruled parallel lines have been etched and filled with black pigment. The two glass plates are cemented together so that the lines cross each other at right angles, forming a uniform grid. The image is focused to the required size as usual, and the half-tone screen is positioned at a specified distance from the sensitive film or plate when the exposure is made. The screen translates the tones of the original into dots of varying size. The light parts of the original reflect light strongly to form relatively large patches of light through the screen openings, and so produce large joined dots on the sensitive surface. Less light is reflected from the greyer and darker tones of the original to produce increasingly smaller dots. The plate is developed

Screens used in the half-tone blockmaking process
1 Normal screen
2 Round screen
3 The screen is used in the reproduction camera to separate the tones of the original into different-sized points

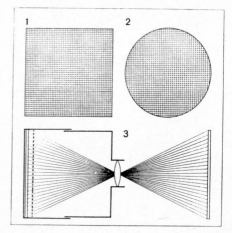

and processed to give a high-contrast dot image.

The half-tone block is produced by copying the negative on to a prepared zinc or copper plate in much the same way as in the line process. Various alternative coating solutions are available to make the light-sensitive coating; they include dichromated process glue, or polyvinyl alcohol, which require subsequent heat treatment to form an etching resist, and the "cold-enamel" coatings made with dichromated shellac, or diazo-sensitized resins, which require little or no heat-treatment. As in the line process the exposure is made in a vacuum frame, usually to arc lamps. The print is developed in water or other appropriate solvent. The plate is then heated if necessary to form the etching resist. Zinc crystallizes and loses its hardness if heated too much, and a "cold-enamel" technique is preferred for this metal.

Zinc plates are etched in nitric acid, and copper plates in ferric chloride solution. The dots are reduced in size by lateral etching, and the process is carried out in stages in which areas where the dots have reached the required size are stopped out with acid-resisting lacquer. This process, called "fine-etching" is used to improve gradation and to alter tone values at the discretion of the etcher. Half-tones on copper are more expensive than on zinc, but the quality is better, and the metal is much harder. The printing life of a copper block is about 150,000 impressions, whereas it is only about 50,000 in the case of zinc.

Powderless etched half-tone blocks

In nearly every up-to-date process house, half-tone blocks are etched by the powderless etching technique. Special etching machines spray the etching solution against the rotating plates. The etching solution contains organic additions which deposit themselves at the flanks of the dots during etching and prevent the etching solution eating into the sides. The resulting dots have the true surface area of the half-tone negative used and a steep clean slope. There is no need to etch in stages. The powderless etching process produces blocks with deep half-tone etchings and the machines allow the production of differently sloped flanks by using different forces of the acid spray.

It may be noted that, since the introduction of powderless etching for the production of large plates for rotary printing, the screen negatives are often made with vignetted contact screens in place of the ruled glass cross-line screens. A vignetted contact screen is made on film (generally by a photographic technique from a cross-line screen), and has a pattern of uniform dot elements, each with a variable density gradient from edge to centre. The screen may be used in the camera, in contact with the sensitive film, or in a vacuum frame, overlaid with a continuous-tone negative or positive. The resulting half-tone image has much the same characteristics as one made with a cross-line screen, but the rendering of fine detail is improved.

Sizes of screen

In the translation of a continuous-tone original into half-tone, the gradation of the tone scale varies somewhat according to the screen ruling. Coarse screens tend to give more contrast but do not render very fine tonal differences so well as fine screens. The choice of screen ruling is governed by the use to which it is put, i.e. the paper on which it is to be printed. The following list shows an approximate relationship of screen ruling to paper:

Screen ruling	Suitable for
45–55	Lowest grades of newsprint.
65–85	Best newsprint and MF paper.
100	Cheap grades of art paper, imitation art and good supercalendered paper.

An enlarged detail from a newspaper picture. The image is virtually obscured by the screen at this degree of enlargement

120	Normal art paper, good imitation art paper, and fine grade super-calendered paper.
133	Good art paper.
150	Finest quality art paper, chromo, and enamel papers.
175	
200	
225	Best quality proofing chromo papers. Not practical for normal printing purposes.

The finer the screen, the better the paper must be. The most widely used screens have from 65–150 lines per inch. There are 22,500 (150 × 150) dots in one square inch of 150-line half-tone block.

Mechanical tints

There are many varieties of mechanical tints composed of dots, lines, and other elements printed on transparent foil which can be applied to an original to give the effect of shading. They are often used directly on line drawings. Techniques are also available for applying tints with "shading mediums" or by photographic means, before etching.

Types of half-tone blocks

There are three main types of half-tone block: squared-up, cut-out, and vignette.

The easiest to produce and most widely used type of block is the squared-up sort. In most cases the blocks are square or rectangular, this being a natural shape

Blocks are attached to a mount to bring them to type height
1 A bevelled block nailed to the mount
2 A block fixed to its mount with a double-sided adhesive foil

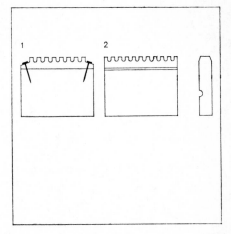

for an illustration. The blocks are trimmed carefully with right-angled corners and flush with the picture when they are to be fixed to the base (to bring them up to type height in the forme) by double-sided adhesive foil. If the blocks are to be nailed to wooden mounts or fixed to proprietory bases, suitable flanges are machined around the edges. The nails can be driven more easily through this flange, and their heads are below type level.

Blocks may also be rounded at the corners, or they may be oval or circular. In cut-out blocks the entire background is either machined or etched away, leaving the subject alone with a sharp contour. In vignetted blocks the background fades gradually away toward the edges. The block has no sharp boundary: the dots on the picture become smaller and smaller until they disappear altogether, leaving the paper white.

Highlight plate

A half-tone block prints the whole picture with varying size dots. With a magnifying glass you can normally see fine dots even in the lightest parts of the picture, and in the darkest parts small white spaces between dots are visible. If all the points were etched or machined from the lightest parts of the block, the highlights of the picture would stand out as empty spaces. And if dark parts of the block had no spaces they would tend to print with a sharp outline which would stand out against the rest of the block.

To print a pencil, chalk or crayon drawing in half-tone and still keep the background free of dots, a modified technique is used. First a normal half-tone negative is made from the original. The screen is then replaced by a clear glass sheet of the same thickness to ensure the same light refraction, and a "no-screen" exposure is made. The white areas on the original become opaque on thenegative and so remain bare after copying on to the zinc plate. They are then completely removed by etching. This is called a "deep-etched" plate or "highlight" plate.

Retouching the original

As we have already seen, fine tone differences are lost in reproduction especially with a coarse screen. This effect can be lessened by retouching the original with a brush or an air-brush beforehand. Dyes or poster colour can be used to strengthen weak parts of the picture and perhaps to tone down parts with too much contrast. Good retouching should be almost unnoticeable. The most difficult retouching work is that on photographs of machines and similar subjects. Often the picture is so heavily retouched and over-worked that very little of the original remains. Sometimes extensive alterations are made to a picture during retouching, but the work is very expensive.

Alterations to the block

Only limited alterations can be made to the block later. Dark areas are lightened by local etching. The correct parts of the block are protected with lacquer and the dark areas are etched with acid. Light areas can be darkened locally by spreading the dots by burnishing.

Colour line reproduction

Solid areas of colour, and colour line subjects are often produced by photo-engraving methods. Effective results are obtained by overprinting two or more line blocks in colour. There are several alternative techniques, but in many cases the artist supplies a key drawing in black, with overlay sheets showing areas where solid or tint (stipple) colours are required. The photo-engraver makes a line block from the line original in the usual way, and produces so-called "bright-prints" on metal from the line negative. He adds the tints where required, paints in the colour areas with an acid resist, and etches the plates. In an alternative method, the artist supplies separate black line drawings for the black and colour plates. Great care is required to ensure perfect registration of the work; it is usual to draw the original for the black plate on white card; the originals for the colour plates are made on dimensionally stable transparent material.

Colour half-tone

Colour reproductions are produced from colour originals, such as colour transparencies of prints, paintings, etc., by multi-colour printing. The four-colour process is generally used, the printing colours being yellow, magenta, cyan and black. The three-colour process, in which the black is omitted, is less expensive, but requires exceptionally good control to obtain results comparable with those given by four-colour printing. It should be noted that many printers still use the older terms "yellow", "red" and "blue" to describe the three printing colours.

The negatives for three-colour reproduction are made on panchromatic films or plates through colour filters which are approximately complementary to the printing colours; that is to say a blue filter (for the yellow printer), a green filter (for the magenta printer), and a red filter (for the cyan printer). The black printer negative for four-colour reproduction is made through a yellow filter, or by successive exposures through the tri-colour filters. Each colour filter transmits only the spectral light or its own colour and absorbs the remainder.

Tone and colour corrections are required, largely to compensate for the spectral limitations of the printing inks, but also to compensate for incorrect colour rendering in the original (especially in the case of colour transparencies), or to meet the requirements of the client. Several alternative masking techniques are available for effecting partial correction; some of them are very complex. In a simple typical method, often used in the reproduction of colour transparencies, a negative mask is made by contact exposure from the transparency on a special photographic film having three colour-sensitive layers, a colour image being produced by dye-coupled development. This mask is superimposed on the transparency when the separation negatives are made through the colour filters. It reduces the density range of the transparency and effects partial correction.

Optical-electronic colour correction methods are also used. In a typical example a colour transparency is scanned by a light spot; the transmitted light is filtered and received by photo-cells to provide signals for the blue, green and red separations. They are fed to a computer where they are corrected, and provide signals at the output to control the optical system for exposing films to make the colour separation negatives or positives.

The half-tone separation negatives are printed down on coated zinc or copper plates which are then etched to provide the colour blocks or plates. The technique is essentially the same as for monochrome reproduction, but further colour corrections are normally made by "colour-etching", a highly skilled form of fine etching. In the past, colour corrections were made entirely by subjective colour etching, without the aid of photographic masking or colour scanning, and in some cases this is still done at the present time. Whatever method is used, the high cost of colour blocks and plates is largely due to the need for tone and colour correction.

Elimination of colour pattern

An objectionable colour pattern or moiré effect would be produced if all colour plates were made with the half-tone screen at the same angle. To avoid this, specially ruled rectangular screens, or a circular screen, must be used. A circular screen has the usual half-tone ruling, but it is turned through a suitable angle (preferably 30 degrees) for each successive exposure when making a colour set. In the resulting

Screens have to be used carefully in making colour blocks
1 A single screen
2, 3 Moire effects caused by super-imposing two screens at the wrong angle.
4 Screens angled at 30° for colour printing

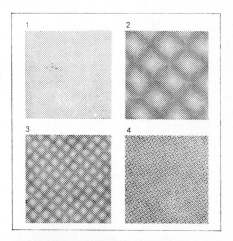

Part of a colour reproduction enlarged. The different coloured dots form a rosette pattern

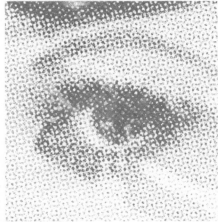

proof the smaller dots do not overlap, but form small rosette patterns (clearly seen with a magnifying glass).

Standard inks have now been widely accepted for tri-colour and four-colour reproduction. The photo-engraver generally makes plates for printing with these inks, which he also uses for proofing. It is not easy to secure good correlation between proofs and printed copies, even when the same paper is used, largely because of the difference in printing speeds, but in any case it is desirable that the printer should use standard inks, otherwise satisfactory colour repro-duction cannot be guaranteed.

Colour prints from black and white

Using special methods with great skill, the photo-grapher and blockmaker can make colour half-tone plates from a black and white original. The method is the same as for a coloured original. Using a rotating screen, four plates are made from the original. These are etched as usual and given to the blockmaker with colour samples or specifications. The blockmaker uses local etching to modify each plate so that they produce a coloured picture when printed together. When this is done with skill and taste, the result is quite convincing.

Altering colour plates

If dots are removed from a black and white half-tone block, empty areas appear on the print. This is not the case with colour plates, where with care, corrections of this type are possible. Where an especially pure tone is wanted, dots can be removed from the black plate by local etching or by machining a larger area. If left, the light-grey tone produced by the dots would deaden the colour. The borders of the removed area must be worked over carefully with an engraving tool. Well executed corrections are hardly noticeable in the final print.

Electronic engraving machines

An electronic engraving machine produces line or half-tone plates directly from the original, without photographic reproduction and etching. A point of light is projected on to the original and the reflection sensed by a photo-electric cell. The impulses are amplified and passed to an engraving head which cuts out parts of the plastic or metal plate according to the tone of the picture. The machine can be set to make plates with dots or line. For a half-tone dot structure the "V"-shaped engraving tool makes deep cuts for the light parts of the subject and shallow cuts for the dark areas. To produce line work, a different type of cutter is used, and a special optical system ensures that when closely spaced lines are located, it cuts less deeply between them than it does in large open areas. Electronic engraving machines are available for enlarging or reducing the scale of reproduction, and for engraving sets of colour plates from a colour original.

Proofs

The printer delivers proof copies with the finished line, half-tone, or colour plates. Unless the customer asks otherwise, these proofs will be on good quality art paper. It often happens that the proof is satisfactory, but that subsequent impressions from the same blocks are a disappointment. There are several possible reasons for this. Often the explanation is that the printer has used a poorer quality paper than for the proofs. To avoid this difficulty, it is advisable to give the blockmaker some sheets of the paper chosen for the main edition when you commission him to make the plates. If the proofs look good on this paper, bad final printing results may be the fault of the printer but some difference must always be expected because printing and proofing conditions are different. For proofs, the plates are inked by hand or mechanically, and the impressions taken at a relatively low speed.

Colour proofs are normally delivered with the original, the plates, details of the colours used, and a note of the order of printing of the plates. All this is to ensure a faithful reproduction. Here we see why the colours for colour printing are standardized, then prints made with the same colours must look the same. The registration marks on the plates must line up accurately if the separate plates are to print correctly. Inaccurate printing produces a blurred picture with coloured borders where the plates have not been in register. "Colour bars" consisting of a photo-engraved solid and (say) a three-quarter tone are often mounted with the plates to assist ink control in proofing. Similar colour bars may be used in printing.

Making duplicates of type or blocks

We may want to take more impressions from type or blocks than the material could stand before wearing out. It is often desirable to print the same subject several times on one sheet at one operation. Better use is made of the machine in this way and time is saved. Several duplicates of the block are needed.

We do not need to repeat the whole block-making process to get these duplicates: there are two methods of producing any number of duplicate blocks from good originals.

Stereotyping

Type pages and coarse screen blocks are usually duplicated by stereotyping. First, a mould must be made from the original. Moist "flong" (tissue and blotting paper adhered together with a special paste) is pressed or beaten into the forme with a stiff brush. The flong is dried and then forms a matrix for the duplicate castings. A disadvantage is that the matrix shrinks a little as it dries, making the final casts slightly inaccurate compared with the original. This is not of great importance in newspaper work, where stereo-types are made of whole sides. The matrix is placed in a casting box powdered with talcum, and a cast is made in metal. The alloy used has a higher proportion of antimony than normal type metal, and is harder and more resistant to wear and tear. After the metal is set, the matrix is pulled away and the stereo is trimmed and planed to type height. Rotary presses need curved

Stages in the making of a stereo:
1 Laying on the flong
2 Beating or pressing
3 Casting the metal
4 The finished casting

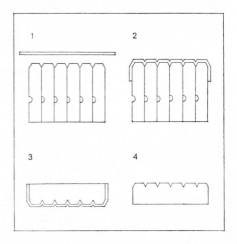

stereos for mounting on the cylinders. These are cast to shape in a curved casting box.

A more involved method, making accurate casts possible, uses "dry flong". Dry flong is a stiff lamination of tissue paper stuck with paste. It is not really dry, but is kept moist until needed. In the same way as wet flong it is beaten or pressed into the forme. The mould is then reinforced by pasting on additional layers of backing paper. The flong is now dried for 10–15 minutes under a hot press, where the matrix cannot shrink. Stereos are cast in the same way as before. With care, up to ten stereos can be made from one matrix.

Alterations and corrections are possible with stereos, especially in pages of type. The affected part is sawn or stamped out of the stereo and a new part soldered in its place. Single letters can be removed and replaced by Monotype letters of the same body size, also soldered in and filed off flush at the back. Sometimes stereos are nickel plated to improve their durability before a long run. Stereo matrices are easy to send by post: they do not cost as much as the much heavier originals or stereos. Picture agencies and news compositors often send matrices of complete articles, advertisements, and pictures to smaller local newspapers and periodicals. In this way the small concerns spare the heavy costs of composition and blockmaking.

Electrotyping

Electrotyping is the most accurate method known for producing duplicates of fine screen half-tone and colour plates. A block of wax or a lead plate about $\frac{1}{16}$ in. (1–2 mm.) thick is laid on the forme, which has first been dusted with graphite. Forme and wax, or lead, are pressed together in a hydraulic press. Wax or lead are used because they reproduce the finest detail, giving a faithful reproduction. The mould is removed from the forme and made conductive by dusting with graphite powder. It then forms the cathode in an electroplating vat, with acid-copper sulphate electrolyte and a heavy copper anode. The electrolytic reaction deposits a shell of copper on the mould. The shell is allowed to grow until it is thick enough, after which it is detached from the mould and backed up with an alloy of lead, tin, and antimony.

Electrotypes give an impression almost undetectable

Making an electro:
1 Laying on the wax block or soft metal
2 Pressing
3 Wax impression in the depositing bath
4 Copper shell
5 The finished electro

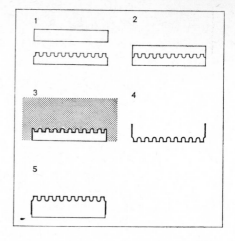

from that of the original, and much sharper than a stereo. To ensure accuracy with colour plates they are all moulded, plated, and backed up together on a single tablet and are separated later. If the plates are too large for this to be done, great care is taken to keep the electrolysis vat at the same temperature, to plate for the same time, and to cast the lead at the same temperature for each plate, otherwise the size of the stereos might differ just enough to give trouble during printing.

Stereos and electros are usually produced 11 pt. thick, but may be delivered bevelled or backed up to type height to special order. By nickel or chromium plating, the durability of the plates can be greatly

A print from a natural form. An electro was first made direct from the fern leaf

increased. A normal stereo will print up to 50,000 copies, and a nickel-plated stereo will print 250,000 copies. A normal electro will print up to 250,000 copies, and a plated electro more than 500,000 copies. The electrotyping process can be used to produce plates from many different materials and originals.

Blocks can also be made from plants and pieces of wood and from textiles and other textured materials. The material to be electrotyped is pressed between a steel slab and the wax or lead. The tablet carrying the impression is used as a mould for an electro in the normal way. The originals of wood- or lino-cuts are often preserved like this by making electros from them. Bookbinders use electros made from blocks for doing embossing work on book cases. These are more robust than usual to withstand the higher pressures; they have a thicker copper shell and a harder alloy backing.

Rubber and plastic blocks

Aniline dye colours, quick drying, and printed from rubber or plastic blocks are more suitable for many types of work, such as packing paper, straw board or paper, and rough or corrugated material. Rubber blocks can be made of type, line blocks, and even coarse half-tone blocks. A laminated sheet of resin-based plastics is pressed against the forme to make a matrix. The matrix is powdered over, and a synthetic rubber cast is taken in a vulcanizing press. The stereos are flexible and can be stuck straight on to the cylinders of a rotary press with double-sided adhesive film.

Polyvinylchloride (PVC) is normally used for plastic blocks which are made in much the same way as rubber stereos, but they are stiff and flat after casting. They must be curved afterwards to fit the cylinders of a rotary press.

Preparations for printing
Making up

The typographic designer receives the proofs from the blockmaker and the text from the printer. Normally he prepares a layout from his first sketchy "rough" and gives it to the printer, who imposes his type accordingly. The compositor reads the corrected text and alters the faulty letters, words, or sentences. The plates must be justified to type height. This may be done by nailing the plate through the bevels to a

Justifying a block to type height:
1 Block
2 Double-sided adhesive foil
3 Mount

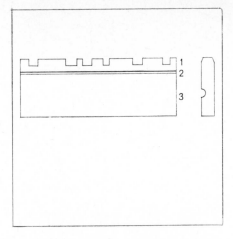

wooden block. Blocks which are to be stereotyped later are mounted on lead, but the great weight is then a drawback. More recently, plastic blocks have been used for mounting plates. A further possibility is to support the plates on pieces of furniture, bound together to form a mount. The plate can be stuck down to the mount with double-sided adhesive material. Plates are made of 16-gauge metal, 0·064 in. (1·6 mm.) thick, and so the mount must not be more than 0·85 in (21·59 mm.) thick. The finished block must be justified to the type height of 0·915 in. (23·37 mm.).

Making ready

The mounted plate is still not ready for printing. It will seldom give an even impression at the first pull. The paper must be pressed evenly against the block and to achieve this the printer underlays the forme with small pieces of paper until a perfect level is attained. This is called "making ready".

First, the printer makes a proof under light or moderate pressure so that he can see where the pressure needs to be increased. Then he underlays the forme where the pressure is light with small, very thin pieces of paper such as tissue paper cut or torn accurately to shape and size. These he sticks in place on an underlay sheet. Making ready must be done very accurately: if the pressure is a tiny bit too much, the ink will be squeezed out around the print. Only by careful work can the printer get the best from the plates. The quality of the final print depends largely on the makeready, underlaid, overlaid or both.

A number of proprietary semi-mechanical make-ready methods have recently come into use which have speeded up the time-consuming normal make-ready. These are predominantly designed to be used as underlays.

Underlaying

For high-quality work both methods of adjustment, overlaying and underlaying, are used. When under-laying, the printer lays card or paper under the forme and blocks and sticks it in place. An underlay need not be renewed each time the forme is used. After use, the forme is coated in vaseline to prevent oxidization and is stored, with its underlay, as "standing matter" until needed again.

Overlaying

Plates mounted on furniture are justified from above. This is called overlaying, and is done by reinforcing the dressing on the cylinder where the pressure is too light. Used in addition to the normal method of paper packing, the chalk relief method is a great help. It limits the amount of "cut and try" work to a minimum. It uses a special chalk coated paper. The printer makes an impression of the forme on this paper with plenty of ink and then dips it in a bath of dilute hydrochloric acid. The ink protects the chalk from the liquid. The chalk dissolves most where there is less ink to form a clear relief in chalk. This chalk relief is stuck on to the dressing on the cylinder. The dressing is the paper or cloth layers covering the platen or cylinder of the press to give the right degree of resilience.

Final preparations

The make-up hand now completes the make up of the book, working to the layout. He now includes the illustrations, the captions, the preliminary pages, and the page numbers. He builds the pages up to their proper size and fills out the spaces with furniture.

The printer receives the finished made up pages and arranges them in a "chase" the size of the sheet to be printed.

Imposition

Imposition means the arrangement of the pages in such a way that they will be in the correct order when printed, folded, and cut. A full sheet normally accommodates

The imposition of a broadside sheet in octavo (8 sheets, 16 pages). The outer form is printed first and the inner forme (pages 2, 3, 6, 7, 10, 11, 14 and 15) second. This second printing is known as perfecting

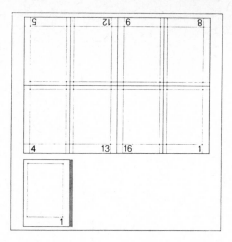

8, 16, or 32 pages, arranged in a special sequence. The printer speaks of the "inner forme" and the "outer forme". If you unfold a folded sheet of paper, one side will be invisible underneath. This is the inner forme. The top visible side is the outer forme. The outer forme is usually printed first (this is called "first printing") and the inner forme second (second printing, backing up, or perfecting). The printer arranges the pages as closely together on the paper as he can, so do not choose a format which does not fit conveniently on the sheet. This leads to poor utilization of the paper, which increases waste and makes the book dearer. Both originals and duplicates, stereos or electros, are used together in the same chase.

Formats

The sizes of the pages are named according to the number of times the full sheet is folded after printing, as follows:

The full sheet is called broadside

Folio (Fol.) 1 fold	2 leaves	4 pages
Quarto (4to) 2 folds	4 leaves	8 pages
Octavo (8vo) 3 folds	8 leaves	16 pages
Duodecimo (12mo)	12 leaves	24 pages
Sixteenmo (16mo) 4 folds	16 leaves	32 sides

The various folding arrangements enable a variety of formats to be obtained from the full sheet (see page 208). As we have seen, the printer arranges the pages as close together as possible. To do this he folds a

The locked-up forme for an octavo sheet

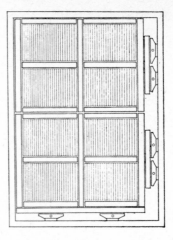

broadsheet and pricks through the corner points of a page, making allowance for trimming. The bookbinder trims the printed pages after binding. About 1–3 ems are trimmed off the three outside edges. The printer unfolds the pricked sheet and measures the distance between the nearest points. He now sets furniture of this width between the pages in the chase, corrects any last errors, and "locks up" the forme in the chase. By wedging the formes tightly in the chase the type is finally secure for printing.

Colour plates must be accurately positioned to give a perfectly registered colour print. The individual plates are generally checked against the first colour sheet. The printer mounts the chase in the machine, checks the makeready on the cylinder, and sets the pressure. The client can ask to check the first impression, or "press proof", and after the machine has been checked and any last-minute corrections to the forme have been made, the printing run can start.

Printing machines

There are three main types of printing machine, or press, as they are called. Of these the "platen press" is the simplest. The forme is held vertically, and is inked by rollers which run down over the type when the hinged platen is opened. When the paper has been inserted, and the platen is closing, the rollers return on to the inking plate. The platen closes and presses the paper against the type and opens again for removal of the printed sheet. On simple jobbing platens the paper may be laid on and taken off by hand. Machine-

Letterpress or Relief Printing

The essentials of the primitive press
1 Platen
2 Paper
3 Type forme
4 Bed

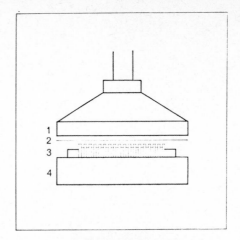

In some old hand presses and proofing presses, the forme is inked by hand

operated platens can print as many as 4,500 sheets an hour. There is a limit to the size of paper which platen machines can print, this being about 15×20 in.

Cylinder presses can work more quickly than platen presses. The type forme is laid on a flat bed which travels under the inking rollers and a rotating pressure cylinder. The paper is laid in a stack in the feedboard of the machine, and sheets are automatically lifted off and placed on the cylinder. The cylinder revolves and presses the paper against the type as it moves by underneath. There are two types of cylinder press: the stop-cylinder and the two-revolution press. The stop-cylinder is so-called because the cylinder stops after each impression to deliver the sheet and to let the bed return to the other end. In the two-revolution press the

The elements of a typical platen press:
1 Paper
2 Platen
3 Inking rollers
4 Forme
5 Bed

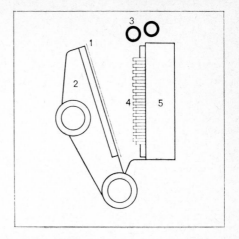

cylinder revolves continuously, rising a little after each impression to let the bed return. To guard against "set-off" (the impression made on the back of sheets of paper by the wet ink from the next) the finished sheets may be interleaved with paper or sprayed with a suitable liquid or powder. Stop-cylinder machines can print up to 3,000 sheets per hour, and two-revolution machines 3,000–5,000 sheets per hour.

The essential difference between cylinder machines and rotary presses is that the former have a flat printing surface and on rotaries it is curved. The cylinder can be changed, complete with stereos, saving much time. Perfecting machines can print both sides of a sheet in one operation. There are two kinds of rotary machine. The sheet-fed rotary, which prints single sheets at the

The elements of a typical flatbed cylinder machine:
1 Paper
2 Impression cylinder
3 Inking rollers
4 Forme
5 Bed
6 Sheet delivery

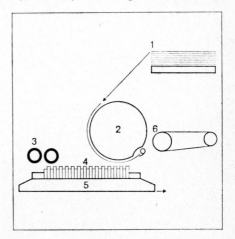

Letterpress or Relief Printing

The elements of a typical sheet-fed
letterpress rotary:
1 Paper
2 Impression cylinder
3 Inking rollers
4 Plate cylinder

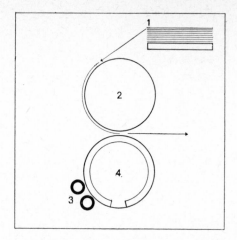

rate of up to 4,000–6,000 per hour, can print sheets of different sizes. The other type, known as web-fed rotary, prints paper direct from the roll and can accommodate only one format. The paper is cut and folded later. These machines can print 10,000–20,000 copies per hour. It is economical to use rotaries only for runs of more than 20,000. Rotaries are used for newspaper and magazine work.

The elements of a typical web-fed
letterpress rotary:
1 Paper roll
2 Impression cylinder
3 Inking rollers
4 Plate cylinder

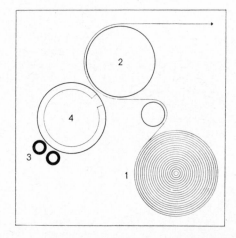

Inking

Even inking is of prime importance for the quality of the printing run. Numerous rollers transfer the stiff printing ink from the ink duct through to the inking table, from where it is carried by distributor rollers and forme rollers to the type surface. The printer can adjust

The operation of a three-rollered inking system:
1 Impression cylinder
2 Inking rollers
3 Forme

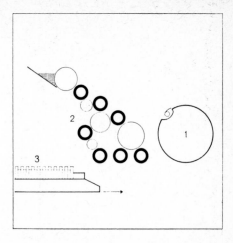

the amount of ink delivered to the type. Too much ink will clog the fine spaces on blocks and type and the ink will dry slowly, bringing the risk of setting off. Too little ink produces a pale, lifeless print. The consistency of the ink is important too. When the ink is too thick, it will pick or pluck the paper. This can be corrected by warming the ink or adding a little varnish.

Aniline printing

Aniline printing is particularly suitable for extremely long runs especially on woody papers, very cheap or thin papers, and also on rough or textured surfaces. Aniline printing uses rubber plates on a rotary press. The inks are spirit based and dry very quickly, allowing rapid printing. The flexible rubber plate presses over the uneven surface and gives an even print.

This process is used for long runs of packaging, wallpapers, cheap envelopes, adhesive labels, and so on.

Printing inks

Letterpress printing inks consist essentially of pigment dispersed in a binding medium such as linseed oil varnish. For colour printing on paper with a non-porous surface the pigment is formulated to dry largely by oxidation. The varnish dries on the surface to form a thin film embedded with grains of pigment. A slow-drying ink is used on porous papers. The greater part of the binder sinks into the paper leaving the rest on the surface to hold the pigment together.

Both opaque and transparent inks are produced for

letterpress printing. Opaque inks cover the colour underneath, whilst transparent inks let the underprint shine through to produce subtractive colour mixing. The printer must know the characteristics of each ink so that he can use it correctly. These are usually printed on each container of ink. The light fastness, alkali resistance, and resistance to varnishing are important.

Light fastness

For work which is exposed to strong light, the ink must be light fast. The ink must not fade, and above all must not change colour. Fading under specified conditions can be measured in the laboratory, but for practical purposes light fastness is sometimes expressed in general terms, the following being typical:

Very good: High standard of resistance to fading; suitable for outdoor exposure.

Good: High resistance to fading for interior exposure for three months.

Fair: Resistance to fading for a few weeks.

Poor: Very fugitive to light.

Resistance to varnish

Book jackets, magazine covers, packages, and similar products are often given a protective coating of varnish. To test the resistance of the ink to varnish, rub a little spirit over a proof. If the colour runs, the ink cannot be varnished. Use exactly the same method with cellulose thinners or acetone to test the suitability of the ink for cellulose varnishing.

Alkali resistance

An alkali-resistant ink must be used on packages for soap, glue, and other alkaline articles. To test the ink for the job, dab a little caustic soda solution on the proof. If the ink discolours it is not alkali resistant.

Pigments

Black printing ink consists normally of carbon powder, gas or lamp black, dispersed in a medium of linseed oil or other varnish. The pigments for coloured inks are made chemically. Various acids and alkalis produce the different coloured pigments from coal-tar varnish. The pigments are ground finely and mixed with the medium to produce the ink.

Metallic printing

In one method of "gold" or "silver" application, an etched plate is used to print a colourless adhesive, and metal powder is dusted over the print while this is still wet. The powder sticks to the adhesive, and the surplus is blown off. Copper, zinc, or aluminium are the metals normally powdered for application in this way.

The application of gold or silver to a picture or page in letterpress and offset is normally done by printing a bronze base, which is a near colourless adhesive varnish. The sheet is then fed through a bronzing machine in which metallic powder—gold, silver or copper coloured aluminium dust—is spread over the whole sheet. The sheet passes under a set of brushes which smooth the metal adhering to the base and remove it where no base is present.

A direct printing of a metallic ink, which is a dispersion of metallic particles in a vehicle, is only successful in gravure where a sufficiently thick layer of the ink can be applied from specially deep etched cells in the gravure cylinder.

In recent years inks with a subdued reflecting appearance have been made for letterpress, offset and gravure by adding extremely fine-ground aluminium dust in limited quantity to normal colour printing inks.

Surface protection

Finished prints can be varnished in any printing machine. The printer loads the machine with spirit or cellulose varnish, replaces the block with a blank plate, and runs the prints through once again. Each print receives an even coating of varnish.

A thin layer of Cellophane offers a more permanent protection against fingering and moisture. A glossy or matt Cellophane film is stuck directly to the print with an adhesive or pure alcohol. Matt films are not suitable for large areas, as they deaden the colour somewhat.

Gumming

Many articles such as labels, stamps, and posters are gummed on the back. Paper may be gummed by hand or in a special machine which rolls a mixture of gum arabic and glycerine on to the paper. Dextrin is more often used nowadays as it is cheaper than gum arabic (page 197).

Linocuts for printing

The simplest form of relief printing is from a linocut. Sometimes linocuts are still used as blocks in letterpress printing for large areas of colour. Work can be printed more cheaply in this way than by any other process. The linoleum is painted with zinc white and pressed against a damp pencil drawing of the picture to be reproduced. The drawing is now in reverse on the lino and the lines can be seen clearly on the white. All the non-printing parts of the drawing are now cut away with different cutting tools, until the printing parts are left in clear relief. Linocuts can be used only as line blocks: half-tones cannot be produced manually.

Embossing and stamping

Embossing is done with solid forms or embossing electros. The tool consists of a matrix and patrix. The card is formed between the two halves under pressure. Round, oval, triangular, and other odd-shaped labels or cards are stamped out by sharpened steel tools. The sheets are stacked, glued across the edges, and cut together in one operation on a special stamping press.

PLANOGRAPHIC AND INTAGLIO PRINTING

Many printers have turned over to planographic printing processes. These differ from letterpress in that the printing and non-printing parts of the block are on the same level. Offset printing is the most widely used planographic process. It is possible to print large even areas of colour easily on posters, maps and similar works.

A great advantage of offset is that it is possible to print with good results on almost any paper from newsprint to fine art paper. A further advantage is that a thin offset plate is easily transportable, and need not be made ready.

Offset has its limitations. Plates for text and lettering are made from films produced on a photo typesetting machine, or they are reproduced photographically from a letterpress proof. Various other "conversion" systems are also available. Once an offset plate is mounted on the cylinder, no alterations can be made as with letterpress. To make alterations or corrections the complete plate must be remade. The range of tones reproduced by offset is more limited than by letterpress, but a good printer can achieve outstanding results from a good original.

Operation of the planographic printing process:
1 Forme
2 Damping
3 Inking
4 Laying on the paper
5 Printing
6 Removing the finished print

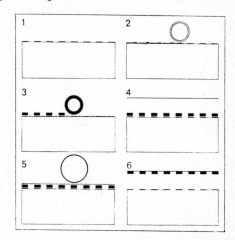

Lithography

The original form of planographic printing is lithography. Lithography is still used as a method of reproducing artists' drawings and paintings in small numbers. It was not until the use of metal as a printing surface was perfected that the planographic process was developed to produce our modern offset for large runs.

Originally, lithography used lithographic stone, which is a form of fine-grained limestone, the best quality coming from the Bavarian quarries. Limestone comes in various grades of hardness. The stone is ground and polished to produce a perfectly smooth level surface, and the design is drawn (laterally reversed) on this with litho drawing ink, using a pen or brush. Drawings with apparent gradation of tone are made with litho chalk or crayon on stone with a grained surface.

When the drawing is finished, the stone is treated with a solution of gum arabic and nitric acid, and dried. Now the surface is rubbed with a solution of asphalt in fatty oils and rinsed afterwards. The drawing appears to have vanished, but in fact the oil has sunk into the stone in the image areas, the other parts being protected by the gum arabic.

The printing depends on the repulsion of water by grease. In the press, rollers damp the stone first. The water soaks into the non-printing parts of the stone and is repelled by the greasy areas. Now the stone is rolled over with printing ink, this taking on the greasy parts, and is repelled by the damp parts. When paper is pressed against the stone an impression is obtained from the inked areas.

It is important that the dampness on the stone is just right. When the stone is too dry, the colour takes a little on the non-printing parts and these no longer print white. When the stone is too damp, droplets of water remain standing on the fatty areas and hinder the even inking.

With skill it is possible to produce colour prints by lithography. Great patience is needed to fit the separate colour designs to one another. As it is difficult to draw a screen on the stone, all the colour mixing is subtractive. "Shading mediums" have a limited application in lithography. Here a hard, gelatine film having a relief pattern of dots, lines or other texture is inked with a roller and pressed against the stone surface. The areas to be kept free are masked out beforehand. By skilful use of different screens it is possible to produce tone gradations.

Offset-litho

Offset-litho printing has taken the place of direct printing, and the plates are mostly made by photo-lithography. Offset printing is used successfully for books, local newspapers, posters and packaging, as well as for many kinds of commercial printing. The original subject is reproduced on the litho plate by techniques somewhat similar to those used for making relief plates for letterpress printing. One important difference is that corrections must be made on the photographic negative or positive; they cannot easily be made on the plate.

Both zinc and aluminium plates are used. The metal surface (except in the case of anodized aluminium) is normally roughened or "grained" to ensure uniform damping in printing. For this purpose the plate is put into a graining machine which consists essentially of a flat tray which is given an oscillating movement by mechanical means. The plate is covered with a layer of glass or steel "marbles" or porcelain balls, together with sand or other abrasive, and water. The movement of the graining machine produces a uniform grain, the character of which varies with the choice of graining materials, the graining time, and other factors.

There are two distinct techniques for producing the image on the metal plate. Using the "surface" or "negative working" method, a line or half-tone negative is made from the original. The plate is coated with a photo-sensitive coating (generally dichromated albumen) or a pre-sensitized plate (prepared for instance with diazo-sensitized resin) may be used. The negatives are copied on to the plate in a vacuum frame by exposure with arc lamp, or similar light source. A fatty ink is applied thinly to the exposed plate which is then treated with water; the unexposed parts of the coating dissolve and are washed away, leaving the image in the form of hardened albumen with a thin covering of fatty ink. From that stage the plate is treated essentially as a drawn or transferred litho plate.

With the "deep-etch" or "positive-working" process, there are two possibilities. A continuous-tone negative may be made from the original, and from this a screen positive is produced. The alternative method is to make a screened negative from the original and produce a contact positive from it. In either case the half-tone positives are retouched for tone or colour correction by "dot-etching" technique. The dots are reduced locally to the required size by the skilled application of hypo-ferricyanide solution ("Farmer's reducer"). Line and half-tone positives are copied on to the sensitized metal plate. The coating in this case is generally dichromated gum. The printing parts of the subjects remain unexposed and are removed during development. The light-hardened gum (after drying) forms a stencil, allowing the image areas to be etched slightly with acid. The metal is only slightly etched at the surface, sufficiently to modify the "grain", ensure good ink receptivity, and longer plate life in printing. The plate is then treated with lacquer and fatty ink to form a litho image in the printing areas, the stencil being removed from the non-printing areas. The plate is gummed-up and made ready for proofing or printing in the usual way.

Type matter can be printed-down to a photo-litho plate from film produced on a photo-typesetting machine. Alternatively it can be reproduced from metal type by one of the "conversion" systems. A well-established method is to make reproduction proofs from the type on transparent plastic or other material in sheet form; they can be printed-down directly in the deep-etch process, or negatives may be made from the proofs for producing "surface" plates. Other methods include the direct photography of the type forme itself, after it has been blackened and then polished on the surface; or the production of repro proofs on special pressure-sensitive material.

Montage

In offset, the whole forme is generally reproduced on the plate in one operation. The imposition stage of letterpress printing is replaced by a montage on clear foil. Half-tone illustrations, line illustrations and type are all arranged and adhered in place on a large transparent sheet. The operator usually lays a sheet of finely-squared paper under the foil to guide him or he may work on a light table with a gridded screen and parallel rules. Various register systems are available for colour work. The printer must be sure that the montage is correct before the litho plate is processed as it is seldom possible to make corrections later. In practice deletions can be made on the plate, but generally nothing at all can be added to the plate.

Proofs

It is usual to take proofs of single or multicoloured illustrations on an offset proofing press. If, on examining the proof, it is decided that corrections are needed, they cannot usually be made; it is necessary to re-touch the negative or diapositive and then make a new plate.

Much depends on the skill of the colour lithographer if a successful print is to be obtained the first time. There is a method for taking pre-proofs from the negatives or diapositives instead of taking a proof from finished plates. A special transparent foil is photo-sensitized and exposed to the negative of the first half-tone colour plate. The resulting image is developed, fixed, and dyed the colour of the ink for this plate. The foil is then re-sensitized and the procedure repeated for the other colour plates. Finally a coloured positive is obtained which approximates in appearance to the final print.

Offset printing

Offset printing is an indirect method. The impression is first made on a rubber sheet or "blanket" from which it is transferred to the paper. The image on the plate must be the right way round. It becomes reversed on the rubber, and finally is the right way up on the paper. The plate is damped before each impression, and this may cause register difficulties with colour prints, as the paper stretches with moisture. In practice good register can be ensured by controlling the moisture content of the paper, and the relative humidity and temperature of the atmosphere. Complete conditioning of the pressroom is desirable.

Originals were sometimes reproduced in six colours to increase the tone range. Thus light blue and light red were added to the usual four-colour set. The offset process is being continually improved so that now it is possible to obtain good results using the three standard colours and black. One disadvantage is that black-and-white pictures lack density in the darker tones but this is sometimes remedied by an additional

Planographic and Intaglio Printing

The elements of a typical sheet-fed
offset rotary:
1 Paper
2 Impression cylinder
3 Rubber blanket cylinder
4 Damping roller
5 Inking roller
6 Plate cylinder

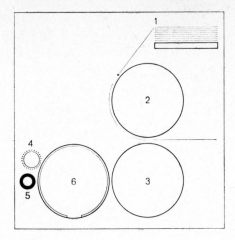

The elements of a typical web-fed offset
rotary:
1 Paper roll
2 Impression cylinder
3 Rubber blanket cylinder
4 Damping roller
5 Inking roller
6 Plate cylinder

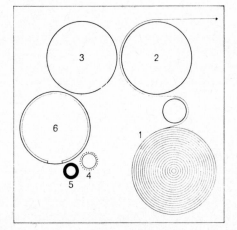

printing on the "Duotone" principle, which uses two
plates. Both reproduce the same picture, but in different contrasts. One plate is soft in tone and is
printed first with a grey ink. The second plate has
more contrast and is overprinted in black to emphasize
the dark tones. This method gives well-modulated
illustrations reproducing all tones of the original
from dense black to lightest grey. Fine lettering,
line drawings and engraved originals print sharply
in offset. This can be seen in maps printed by offset
lithography.

Offset can be used for a wide range of work: it can
print on newsprint as well as on cartridge or on
coated papers. Another advantage is the practicability
of the light metal plates, which are often larger than

letterpress formes. Offset presses are built for 1 to 6 colours and also to perfect.

The main differences between an offset press and a letterpress rotary are the addition of an extra cylinder with the rubber blanket, and the provision of a damping unit in addition to the inking rollers. On a two-colour press, which has four cylinders, the two colours can be printed directly after one another in a single transit. Sheet-fed offset rotaries can print up to 10,000 copies an hour, and single or multi-colour reel-fed machines can deliver up to 20,000 and more. Normally the plates are regrained for re-use after printing, so it is as well to arrange with the printer to store the plates if you think you may need reprints. Otherwise the printer keeps only the films from which he can make new plates if necessary.

Transferring

Designs done in other processes can be transferred to offset or lithographic plates. A print is taken from the original wood- or linocut, line block, or engraving, on transfer paper. The ink impression is transferred to the offset plate under pressure. The plate is processed in the usual lithographic manner. This method is also used to duplicate plates, and to make multiple images on plates. The transfers are adhered to a backing sheet in the correct position for transfer to the new plate. Photographic and other "conversion" techniques have now largely replaced the traditional transfer methods.

Small offset printing

This simplified offset process, using small easily operated machines, is suitable for medium runs. It needs no specially trained operators. By virtue of its low costs, the process is suitable for office use. It enables the office to print its own work. The plates are prepared paper or thin aluminium sheets. They can be imaged in a normal typewriter using a special ribbon, or it is possible to draw or write directly on the plate with a grease crayon or special ink. The plate is then wiped over with a sponge soaked in a "fixing" solution (essentially gum arabic) and is ready for use when dry. The process can be used to print on all grades of paper, from airmail sheets to card.

It will also print rough-surface papers. By using a

photosensitive plate, line blocks, type formes, and black-and-white or colour photographs can be reproduced. These presses will produce up to 9,000 prints an hour and will take sheets up to about 15×20 in.

Collotype

A planographic process which is very seldom used today is collotype. This is the only process by which a black-and-white or coloured continuous-tone can be produced without using a screen and at the same time gives good quality reproduction. The process is used now chiefly for reproducing paintings for artistic publications. The secret of the process is the fact that a film of gelatine and potassium bichromate hardens when exposed to light and, after damping with water, takes ink only on the hardened parts.

Making the plate

A continuous-tone negative is made from the original. For colour printing, colour separation negatives are made. Colour corrections are carried out on the negatives by hand retouching. If several illustrations are to be printed on one plate, a transparent montage is made as for offset.

The printing plate is a sheet of thick glass, finely ground on one side and coated with a substratum and a sensitive solution of gelatine and potassium bichromate. The coated plate is dried and "baked" at a moderate temperature in a "Collotype oven". The baking modifies the physical characteristics of the gelatine so that a "reticulated" grain forms. The plate

An enlarged section of a reticulated plate

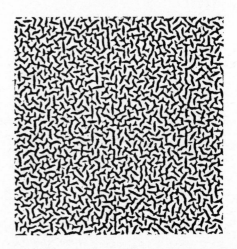

is exposed to the negative, the gelatine hardening in proportion to the amount of light received. The plate is washed to remove remaining potassium bichromate and then dried.

Before use, the plate is coated with a mixture of glycerine and water. The film then retains the moisture in varying degrees according to how much light it has received. The amount of ink retained is governed by the graduation of moisture in the plate.

Printing the plate

The plate must be kept moist by repeated applications of glycerine and water. The plate is inked and the ink is printed on the paper under pressure. The Collotype hand press is similar to the old type lithographic press, and is hand operated. Flat-bed machines similar to the old type of litho machines are also used. Printing is slow and only about 1,000–1,200 copies can be taken from one plate. This run sometimes takes two or three working days to complete. However, the process is capable of giving better colour prints than any other method, and this justifies its use in printing small but variable runs of reproductions of paintings or de luxe editions.

Intaglio and Photogravure

Intaglio printing is used to a limited extent for bank-notes, share certificates, postage stamps and high quality calling and greeting cards. The design is hand engraved or etched into the smooth plane surface of the printing forme. For printing, the forme is covered

Enlarged detail of a photogravure plate. The deeper cells at the bottom print a darker tone than the shallower cells above

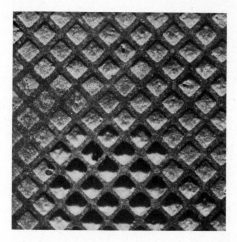

Enlarged detail of a photogravure print

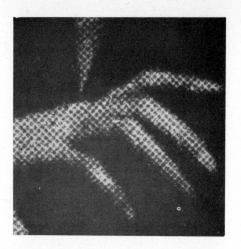

completely with a stiff ink, which is then wiped off the plate surface leaving ink only in the recesses forming the design. A print is obtained by applying pressure to the back of the paper placed on the forme.

Photogravure is the industrial high speed system of intaglio printing using a copper cylinder as printing forme into which a design is etched. The cylinder turns in a shallow trough filled with liquid gravure ink. The removal of the surface ink is effected by a knife edge called a doctor which is pressed against the cylinder surface. To keep the doctor in the plane of the cylinder surface over large etched areas, a fine system of cross lines is left in all etched areas during etching and forms a system of cells of different depth. Shallow cells containing only a minute volume of ink print light tones and deeper cells are produced where darker tones are to be printed. In this way photogravure allows a real variation of tone values to be printed.

One advantage of rotary photogravure is the great reduction in the cost of printing large editions. The cost of cylinder preparation is however relatively high, and for this reason the minimum economical run is generally of the order of 50,000 copies. The printing cylinder forms a complete unit (i.e. it is not segmented), and this means that once it is etched, no substantial alterations or corrections can be made.

The quality of photogravure varies with printing conditions. Normally the pictures have rich shadows and good middle-tone gradation, but retouching is necessary to ensure really good light-tone rendering. Monochrome or colour photogravure printed on uncoated papers is almost invariably better than letter-press printed on similar papers, and it compares very favourably with offset-litho printing. At the same time, type matter is not so well reproduced by photogravure, because the characters are cut across by the screen lines, and this gives a slight "saw-tooth" edge to them. As in the other processes, the type may be printed-down from photo-typeset films, or it may be produced by one of the "conversion" systems.

Photogravure cylinder production

In the conventional process (which is called depth variable), continuous-tone and line negatives are made on the reproduction camera. They may be retouched if desired. Contact positives are then produced from the negatives, and they are normally retouched. Various photographic masking, or electronic scanning methods are available for colour correction, although further modifications are often made by hand retouching. Most of the retouching is carried out by the skilled application of dye, while tones may be lightened by normal photographic reduction methods, and high-lights may be emphasized by knife-work. The image in the positives must be regarded as final; only minor corrections can be made on the cylinder.

Coloured originals are reproduced by printing from four cylinders in yellow, magenta, cyan and black, as in the other processes; good results can be obtained by tri-colour reproduction (without black), but for various technical reasons this is seldom done in practice. The negatives for colour work may be made on glass plates or on dimensionally stable film; the latter is preferred for the positives.

The positives are mounted or "planned" on trans-parent plastic material over a lay-out sheet on a light table, as for offset-litho. The assembly of positives is contact printed on to "carbon tissue" which consists essentially of a coating of gelatin on a paper base, sensitized with potassium dichromate. A special form of photographic film may be used alternatively. An exposure is first made under a photogravure screen, which has two sets of clear lines crossing at right-angles on an opaque background. The usual rulings are 150–175 lines per inch. The purpose of the screen exposure is to divide the image into small elements which, when etched in the cylinder, hold the printing ink better than wide recesses. The second exposure is made under the assembly of positives. As in the other processes, the exposures are made in a vacuum frame, to arc lamps or similar light sources. A photo-chemical action takes place in which the gelatin is differentially hardened to a degree which depends on the amount of light received through the screen and through the continuous-tone positives.

The cylinders are prepared by electro-deposition of copper on a base of steel (or in some cases, alumi-nium). A substantial layer of copper may be deposi-ted, to be afterwards ground and polished to provide a smooth level surface. Alternatively a thin skin of copper is deposited on a smooth base; it only requires polishing, and can be stripped on completion of the job.

The carbon print, which has been made by exposure under the screen and positives, is transferred on to the cylinder by the application of cold water and rolling pressure. The print is "developed" in warm water, the paper backing being removed, and the soluble gelatin washed away to leave a relief image of hardened gelatin on the cylinder to form an etching resist. The resist is dried, marginal areas are protected with asphalt varnish, and the cylinder is etched in solutions of ferric chloride. The rate at which the etchant penetrates the resist and etches the underlying copper depends on the thickness of the gelatin and the concentration of the solution. In practice a series of etching solutions of progressively decreasing con-centration are used to produce a graded etching.

Tone and colour corrections are sometimes made on the cylinder, generally after proofing, by rolling-up with stiff ink and local etching. Hand-engraving and electro-deposition techniques are also used. The cylinders are usually chromium-plated to increase their durability. It is generally considered that, under good conditions, up to about 100,000 copies can be printed from the bare copper. The life of the cylinder is very much increased when it is chromium plated, and the chromium deposit can be renewed if it shows signs of wear.

Area variable and area-depth variable gravure

Photogravure cylinders made by the "conventional" process generally have excellent quality, but the technique requires considerable skill, and there is difficulty in printing exceptionally large editions be-cause of the action of the doctor blade in conjunction with the paper which slowly wears away the doctor bearing cell walls and effectively reduces the depth of the highlight cells. This leads to a loss of highlight details in the print.

As the volume of the ink in the cells determines the printed result, it is an advantage for long-run gravure to use a half-tone gradation where the light tones are printed from cells with a small volume of ink. This is effected by using deep cells of small surface area. Special photographic procedures or vignetted gravure contact screens have to be used to create the required gravure area-variable half-tone positives which can be transferred to the cylinder by conventional carbon tissue transfer or directly on light sensitive coated copper cylinders. These area-variable processes are used for packaging and other forms of specialized printing. For very high quality gravure printing, the area-variable method raises problems on account of the very small surface area of the highlight cells, which are difficult to print on paper. For high quality long run gravure magazines, travel brochures and mail order catalogues a double-positive process is used, requiring the conventional continuous tone positive and, in place of the gravure screen exposure of the carbon tissue, a second exposure under an invert half-tone positive in which the highlight dots are considerably larger than for a single positive method. The resulting etching contains cells in which the tone values are represented by cells having varying depth and varying surface areas.

Electronic engraving technique

The principle of the electro-mechanical engraving of letterpress blocks and litho positives has been applied to the production of gravure cylinders. In conventional gravure the cells are all square and of the same size but vary in depth according to the required tone value. In the engraving machine an angular stylus cuts more or less deeply into the rotating cylinder surface creating cells in the form of inverted pyramids. The resulting gravure cell formation is therefore area and depth variable. The stylus gets its energy from electrical impulses caused by scanning a positive or negative reflection copy of the job which is mounted on a cylinder turning and moving in complete synchronisation with the cylinder to be engraved.

Photogravure printing

The principle of photogravure printing may be described by reference to a much simplified machine. In one design, the cylinder is mounted in the machine with its lower part revolving in a trough of ink. Generally a fairly liquid ink, made with a fast drying solvent, is used. A thin flexible steel blade, called the "doctor", wipes off excess ink, leaving the non-printing areas, and the tops of the screen walls free of ink, while the recesses are full. The paper, or other printing material (foil, plastic, etc.) is fed between the cylinder and a roller covered with hard rubber to which considerable pressure is applied. The ink is transferred from the depressions in the cylinder to the printing material. Differences in tone value are caused by the fact that the deep recesses contain more ink than shallow ones. The screen lines serve only to support the doctor as it wipes off the excess ink. In half-tone photogravure gradation of tone is due to differences in the area of the dots, or (in the two-positive process) to differences in both area and depth.

Reel or web-fed gravure presses are used for long runs of magazines, packaging, travel brochures and other matter requiring plenty of strong colour pictures. Modern presses produce 20–30,000 copies per hour and consist of a multitude of units, one for each colour. To print products with full four-colour pictures on both sides of the web, an eight-unit press is required, and often for high pagination products several of such groups have to work together into a common folder. To achieve the high speed of modern

Operation of the intaglio printing process
1 Forme
2 Inking with the "doctor" removing excessive ink
3 Laying on the paper
4 Printing
5 Removing the print

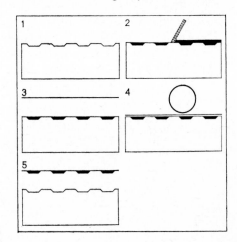

processes, it is necessary to lead the web after each printing unit into a dryer, to assist the drying of the volatile ink by a strong often warmed air blast before the print reaches the next printing point. The drying hoods enable the drawn-off solvent to be collected for re-use and are instrumental in preventing the escape of solvents into the atmosphere.

Rotary sheet-fed machines are used for high quality work and smaller editions. Normal printing speeds are about 5,000–8,000 impressions an hour. But more and more work of this nature is now captured by offset. Sheet-fed machines taking etched copper plates, instead of cylinders, are used to a limited extent; this method, attractive in principle, has various technical difficulties which have restricted its development.

Elements of a typical sheet-fed gravure
rotary:
1 Paper
2 Impression cylinder
3 Plate cylinder
4 Ink trough
5 Doctor

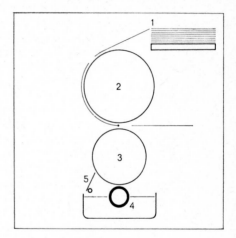

Elements of a typical web-fed gravure
rotary:
1 Paper roll
2 Impression cylinder
3 Plate cylinder
4 Inking trough
5 Doctor

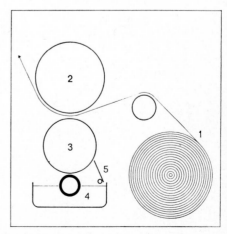

CRAFT PRINTING

There are many less complicated methods of producing designs, illustrations and occasional lettering. These can conveniently be labelled craft printing methods, although some of them have developed beyond that stage.

Woodcuts

The art of woodcutting was already practised in the first half of the fifteenth century for reproducing writing and illustrations, even before Gutenberg's invention of movable types. The first woodcuts were cut along the grain. You can recognize the grain in the finished print. The lines of the illustration were partly dictated by the run of the grain.

Around the end of the eighteenth century, a swing started toward cutting across the end of the grain. This new technique made it possible to print fine lines, and even to achieve a degree of tone by "hatching" or cutting fine lines across one another to print a coarse grid. Boxwood was normally used.

Later still, with the coming of photography, it was possible to coat the wood with a light-sensitive layer and to transfer the picture photographically. The wood

Detail from a Polish woodcut
(*The Last Supper*) c. 1750-1850

was then cut by hand or on a machine making parallel or even concentric cuts. Xylography, or mechanical wood engraving, was born.

Before the coming of the etched metal plate, xylography was the most perfect method of reproducing black-and-white and coloured originals. Many of the woodcuts of those times appear naïve to us, with their stiff representations of figures and objects. Modern copies in the same style, are sometimes used as vignettes or as humourous features in graphic and advertising design.

Engraving methods

True *woodcuts* are engraved along the grain using a well planed and smoothed piece of beech, pear, or cherry wood. The character of a true woodcut comes from the movement of the knife, greatly influenced by the direction of the grain which makes cutting across it more difficult. To make the structure of the wood more marked, roughen the surface by firm brushing with a wire brush along the grain before cutting.

Wood engravings are cut across the end of the grain. The best wood to use is box. Large blocks must be glued together in sections. Special tools are available but wood engravings can be made with a copper engraver's graving tool.

Transferring the drawing

You can draw directly on the smooth surface of a wooden block. To make the lines more visible, coat the surface with chalk primer or roll on a coat of zinc white printing ink a few days before use. You may dust the ink with talcum.

Another way is to trace the drawing straight through from tracing paper. Tape the drawing face-down on the block and lay a sheet of carbon paper underneath it. Draw round the outlines with a hard pencil and you will have a clear drawing on the primed block.

A simpler method is to transfer the drawing directly using gummed paper. Make the drawing on the gummed side of a sheet of sticky paper and lay the paper, drawing down, on the block and pin it in place. To moisten the gummed paper, lay a sheet of damp blotting paper over the back. Weigh this down with another block of wood and put the whole in the press. Wait a minute for the water to soak through and then increase the pressure. When you pull off the layers of paper, the drawing will remain on the face of the block. You can make your own gummed paper with dextrin glue and thin paper, or you may buy it from a shop.

Cutting

Cut the design about $\frac{1}{16}$ in. deep in the wood so that the printing parts remain standing. There are several different shaped tools for wood-cutting, each mounted on a wooden handle: the graver and the lining tool, the round graver and round gouge, the flat gouge, the screen graver, and the angled blade. The lining tool is for cutting fine lines, and the round and flat gouges for removing large areas. The screen graver is for cutting fine parallel lines. Another tool is used to make two parallel cuts to take out a V-shaped section of wood.

Woodcutting tools:
1 Vee cutter
2 Round gouges
3 Chisel
4 Screen graver
5 Angled chisel

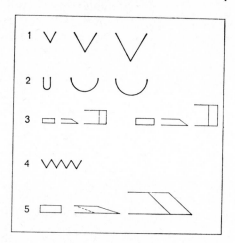

It is a good idea to lay the wood block on a round sandbag, so that you can turn it in all directions. Hold the block with your left hand and cut away from yourself with the tool in your right hand. Never cut toward the hand holding the block: this can lead to serious wounds when the tool slips.

Linocuts

Linoleum is an excellent material to handle, and is equally suitable for all types of work. You can obtain linoleum in large-sized pieces, so it can be used for posters, large coloured areas and also for posters with negative lettering.

Linoleum about $\frac{1}{8}$ in. (3·5 mm.) thick is best for linocuts. There are two types of linoleum, one containing cork filler, and a cork-free variety. You can make clean-edged cuts in cork-free linoleum, but the edges will always crumble a little in the other sort, and the print displays slightly rough outlines. This effect is often used intentionally, but it is only to be recommended for larger designs.

To cut the size of sheet you need from the roll or sheet, mark out the edges on the back and cut through the cloth backing first. You can easily break the lino along the cut. Prime the linoleum and transfer the drawing in the same way as described for woodcuts.

You can use the same woodcutting tools for lino work, but you can also obtain very useful sets of special lino-cutting tools. In each set a variety of small nib-like tools are mounted on wooden holders. They are very practical to use.

Lettering in linoleum

Give the lino block a coat of zinc white, dust it with talcum if you wish, and leave it to dry. Take a pull of the composed type on paper in a hand press, lay it face-down fresh on the whitened lino, and press the two together in the press. When you have carefully pulled away the paper, you will see the lettering in reverse on the lino surface. Engrave the reversed lettering into the surface. Be careful not to "undercut" the block, so that the outlines of the design remain unsupported, or they will not print properly. The best cut is at right-angles to the surface. Work around rounded lines with a round gouge. Mount the finished block and justify it to type height.

Undercutting on line blocks can cause
detail to break away
1 An undercut line block
2 A correctly cut block

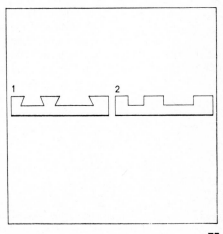

Lead engravings

You can do very finely detailed work with the same tools on a sheet of lead. It is also possible to do fine engravings on lead. You can make very clean cuts in lead as the material is helpful, unlike wood and linoleum where parts may break away and spoil your work, unless you can put this characteristic to artistic use. It is possible to fill in mistakes on a lead block with solder and to scrape them level again. You must sharpen the knives frequently on a stone to get uniform clean cuts. You can order the lead plates the size you want them from a stereotype caster.

Engraving on plastic

Remarkably fine cuts are possible on sheets of P.V.C. (polyvinylchloride) floor covering, which is similar to linoleum. The material is usually only about $\frac{1}{16}$ in. (2 mm.) thick, so take care not to cut right through or pieces will begin to fall out of the design. You can also use celluloid, cork, leather, or rubber blocks to make good cuts. Use a hard rubber, keep the knife sharp, and moisten it from time to time.

Mounting wood, lino, and lead cuts

If you intend to take prints from the blocks in a platen press, you must mount them type high, the same as all other printing pieces (see page 18). It is possible to adjust the height of the platen, but it is preferable to justify the wood block by underlaying it with board or layers of card. Glue linocuts on to a wooden block or furniture and then justify it as usual. Universal glues or double-sided adhesive foils are suitable for this job.

When cutting coloured lino blocks, take a print from the first colour block on the gum side of gummed paper and press this wet on to white primed lino for the second block. Note carefully which block prints which colour. The parts of the block which appear in the print must remain standing; the other non-printing parts must be removed. Cut large non-printing areas right out of the block to guard against the danger of it printing accidentally. For $\frac{1}{4}$ in. thick linoleum use $\frac{3}{4}$ in. thick board or type furniture as a mount and justify to type height with paper or card.

Printing wood and lino cuts

Before printing with a wood- or linocut roll the colour on to the block with a hand roller. The raised parts of the block are inked and the recesses remain clear. The simplest way of taking a print is to lay a clean sheet of paper on the block and to roll over the back with a clean hand roller or to press the paper down evenly with a folding bone. Lift the sheet carefully and you will have a clean print on the paper. You can print coloured blocks in this way.

Printing is more convenient in a hand or proofing press. Lay the block on the bed, ink it, and lay a sheet of paper in place, and cover it with about six sheets of scrap. Wind the bed under the platen and put on pressure with the lever. The print is made in exactly the same way as proofs are taken from a type forme.

Any paper which does not pluck or dust is suitable for printing (see page 192). Every little inaccuracy, even the roughness of the linoleum surface will show on art paper, whereas they disappear on a rougher paper, especially when you use a little more ink. When printing a run on a lino block, always use a little more ink than normal. With good blocks, you should be able to print up to 25,000 copies without the quality deteriorating noticeably.

You may increase the resistance of the linoleum block to wear by giving it a coat of shellac before printing.

By overprinting transparent inks with lino blocks you get subtractive colour mixing. Print the lighter colours first, and finish with the darkest. You can only print the next colour when the previous one is dry.

Printing inks are eminently suitable for lino printing. For short runs, printed by hand pressure, lino printing water colours are useful. These colours are water based and can be applied with a roller as oil colours. Linocut water colours can be mixed with one another.

You should use a porous paper with these colours such as Chinese rice straw paper or Japanese wood paper. Alternatively you may use Ingres or moulded paper. Wet the sheet with a sponge and press it lightly between two sheets of blotting paper or newsprint. When it is only damp lay it over the inked block, cover it with a sheet of scrap paper and apply even pressure over the back with a hand roller or folding bone. The light paper absorbs the colour readily and can soon be lifted off. Protect the finished prints from moisture.

Printing without blocks

To make a print of wood texture take a soft wood such as spruce or pine cut as a block or veneer. Roughen the surface by firm brushing with a wire brush along the grain until you can feel the texture. You can take prints from the wood in the normal way after inking with a roller.

Textiles can be printed in a similar manner. Cut a piece of cloth to size and glue it on to a piece of linoleum and justify the block to type height. Skin or bone glues, or resin glues are best for this job (see page 195). Impregnate fibrous substances with shellac or waterglass before printing.

In the same manner you can print many textures such as woven fabrics, nets, and natural designs like autumn

A print from a piece of spruce

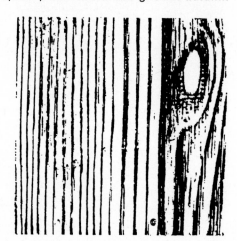

leaves, and blades of grass. Use a soft underlay such as linoleum. Ink the structure well with a roller and print it with hand or mechnical pressure on to a clean sheet of paper.

Stencilling with paper masks

This technique is suitable only for single prints, but is very useful for poster designs and similar large exercises. We could almost describe the method as a planographic printing process. First cut a paper stencil, to cover the negative parts of the design, with a trimming knife or tear it to shape. You may reinforce the stencil with a thin wide mesh gauze or net. Ink a sheet of linoleum of the required size with a printing ink and lay the stencil on the wet colour. The ink will hold the stencil in place. Now lay the paper for the print over the block and roll over the back with a hand roller or put the whole in a press. All the areas not covered by the stencil will print on the paper.

To save colour when the blank areas are large, lay the stencil on the uninked linoleum and roll on the colour over the stencil. The lino will carry ink only where the stencil was open. Clean the lino sheet with trichlorethylene or benzine and it is ready for the next print. You can also print plant or leaf forms using this method. Lay the material on the linoleum and ink over the whole plate, and carefully lift off the plant. This leaves an uninked area on the lino which prints negative on the paper. To obtain a positive print, ink the

A print made with positive and negative paper masks

subject first, press it evenly on to the lino block, and then lift it away. Put the paper over the inked area and take a print as normal.

Glass prints

Glass prints are useful for design work, and produce only a single copy. They are done in oils and show a marked brush texture. Paint and draw your design in reverse with oil colours on a large sheet of glass. To emphasize the special characteristic of glass prints, use a stiff brush, and do not lay the colour on thickly. There must be no thick daubs of paint: these will squeeze out to give ragged outlines on the paper. If the colour is too hard, thin it with a little linseed oil or varnish. You can paint as many different colours on

Craft Printing

A glass print. The oil colour was laid on
the glass with a palette knife

the one design as you like. Use a porous paper for the
print. Lay it over the drawing on the glass and work
over the back with a hand roller under firm pressure
until you think all the colour has been taken up. Pull
the paper away carefully and the drawing will be
printed on it.

Potato blocks

This is a method similar to lino cutting, principally
useful for printing repeating designs or doing designs
for endpapers or wrapping paper. Wash a large potato
and cut it in half. Draw the design in reverse on one of
the flat faces. A copying pencil is best for this. Cut
away the negative parts with a knife, leaving the design
in relief. Cut simple decorative forms like squares and
circles from a narrow strip of potato. Print the design
by hand, loading the stamp with tempera colour from
a brush. It is easier to spread the colour on a glass
plate and to stamp the block alternately on the glass
and paper.

SILK SCREEN PRINTING

We could have included silk-screen printing under craft printing because it is a process which every pictorial designer can use himself. Nowadays, however, it is extensively used for quite long runs on a variety of materials and is an important branch of the printing industry.

Nevertheless, silk-screen is often the only economical process for short runs of large designs. It can be used to print on all papers and also on a wide range of materials such as wood, metal and plastic on curved or flat surfaces. It can duplicate coloured posters, lettering, chalk drawings for book jackets, pen drawings, brush drawings, and even natural structures. The process offers a whole range of design possibilities which can hardly be bettered for speed and clarity by any painting, drawing, or even montage method. You yourself can make single prints or do short runs without any great knowledge and at no great cost. The following description explains the most important points to enable you to make use of the method.

Printing frame

The printing frame consists of a wooden frame over which is stretched a fine silk, nylon, bronze, or steel

Elements of the silk-screen process:
1 Uncoated screen
2 Coated screen with masks
3 Positioning the paper
4 Spreading the colour with a squeegee
5 Removing the screen

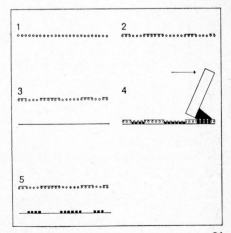

Silk Screen Printing

A simple silk-screen printing table:
1 Frame
2 Hinges fixing frame to table
3 Screen
4 Squeegee with support rods

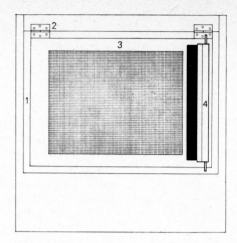

Paper positioning on the silk-screen printing table:
1 Raised frame
2 Lay marks for the paper
3 Paper

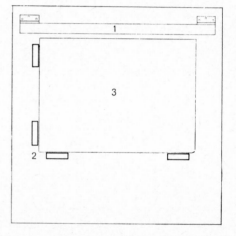

gauze. There are many different-sized frames. The stencil is put on the screen in a variety of ways. The stencil blocks out the areas which do not print on the design and stops the colour coming through the screen while leaving the printing parts open. The tacky ink is drawn over the screen with a squeegee and is pressed through the open parts on to the paper. The texture of the mesh becomes almost invisible.

Making the stencil

The type of stencil used depends on the application and above all on the kind of ink to be printed. The simplest to make is a glue stencil, which is suitable for all applications except those using water-soluble inks.

82

Glue stencil

You can make a glue stencil in two different ways. Lay a protective transparent sheet over your drawing and place the screen over it. Over all the areas of the drawing which should not print, paint the surface of the screen with a water-soluble cold glue. Fish glue is best for the work. When the screen is dry it is ready for printing. The following method is more accurate: print or draw over the printing parts of the design on the screen with lithographic ink or oil crayon. Now coat the whole of the surface of the screen with fish glue. You may have a specially designed container for this, which covers the whole of the screen at one pass, but with a little skill you can lay on an even coat with a strip of stiff card. When the glue is dry, wash out the lithographic ink or crayon with a sponge and turpentine from the surface of the screen. Rinse the screen with a little benzine afterwards.

Cut-out stencils

A cut-out stencil is the best for accurate designs composed with straight lines. The stencil paper used consists of two layers lightly held together: a thick base paper, and a thin, usually transparent, adhesive coated paper forming the stencil itself. The adhesive is generally shellac or a synthetic resin glue. Carefully cut the lines of the design in the thin stencil paper. You may work freehand or use a ruler and cutting compass. You must remove the printing parts of the stencil.

Iron the finished stencil on to the underside of the screen with a medium-hot iron. The warmth melts the shellac which then binds the screen and paper. When using synthetic resin adhesive papers lay the stencil under the screen and wipe over the inside of the gauze with a sponge soaked in solvent. The solution softens the resin and the stencil sticks to the screen. The screen is ready for printing as soon as you have re-moved the base paper. You can also print water-soluble colours with this preparation.

To remove the stencil simply wash the screen down with the correct solvent. This is usually methylated spirit or commercial shellac remover, or acetone or cellulose thinners for a resin glue. It is advisable to make each successive stencil for a colour print from a print of the last stencil, to ensure correct alignment and thus an accurate print. You will save much trouble by including small registering crosses at the corners of the original and again on each new screen.

Direct photographic stencils

The photographic stencil is universally applicable for sharply contoured lettering, for flat areas, and also for pen and brush drawings. The screen is sensitized with a solution of gelatine and potassium or ammonium bichromate. You can buy this solution in its components to be mixed just before use. Spread the solution evenly on to both sides of the gauze with a strip of card or better, with a special angled container. This container can be tipped to retain or discharge its contents over a long straight lip. Hold the screen vertical and,

Coating a silk-screen with a spreader:
1 Start
2 Tip and draw upwards (the gelatine flows forward on the screen)
3 Finish

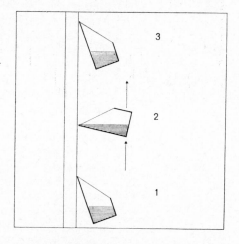

start at the bottom, tip the container forward so that the solution flows against the gauze and draw it through to the top. At the top tip the container so that the remaining solution runs back into the container. If the screen is wide you may have to repeat this precedure more than once on each side. Dry the screen horizontally, laying it across two chair backs or trestles.

You must do the coating and the drying by subdued light. In a room lit by daylight you can filter the light by hanging or stretching a yellow plastic sheet across the window to make sure that the gelatine layer is not prematurely hardened by exposure to light. You may accelerate the drying with a medium warm draught from a hair dryer or heater. The remaining mixed solution will keep a few weeks in a dark brown container, but if you use only a little at a time it is better to mix it as you need it.

Sunlight exposed stencils

If you have not got a copying apparatus the following method will bring good results. Draw the design, not in reverse this time, on the inside of the screen with masking paint. This is water soluble and is usually red. Expose the screen outside in daylight, 10–20 minutes in the sun or 20–30 minutes if the sky is cloudy. Place the inside of the screen toward the sun and stretch a sheet of black paper over the back of the screen. The paper should be in good contact with the screen to avoid any light being reflected on to the back of the design. This would harden the gelatine layer on the back of the design. Press the paper against the screen with a drawing board and clamp the two firmly together with G-clamps. The gelatine hardens on the negative, exposed, areas and thus becomes water insoluble. Wash the unexposed parts away later with warm water and dye the remaining areas to make the stencil more plainly visible. Make any necessary corrections with shellac. You can now print oil-varnish-, lacquer-, or water-based colours through the screen.

A further interesting possibility is the following: coat both sides of the screen in the usual way and expose it to sunlight or daylight until the coating takes on a brown tint. Now draw your design on the screen with a pen or brush and screen drawing ink, a strong potassium permanganate solution. The solution decomposes the gelatine coating which turns a dark brown. You will easily see this happening. Now dust the screen well with bisulphide powder or brush it over with bisulphide solution and then wash it in water. The decomposed areas are now open and the screen is ready for printing. Use only fine screens for delicate drawings. You can correct small mistakes with varnish.

Making a screen with printing frame

If you have a printing frame you can make screens from normal diapositives as line drawings, coarse half-tones, or even from lettering printed on clear foil. You can also make a drawing on a translucent plastic sheet, matt on one side. It is preferable to use completely clear foils: the opaque paint holds well and the matt surface does not affect the copying process at all. The diapositives are held against the screen by a vacuum arrangement and the whole exposed to strong light from behind the screen. The lamps are usually fluorescent or arc lamps. Vacuum frames are very expensive and are generally only economical for commercial printers. Any large silk-screen printing works will copy a diapositive on to a screen for you.

Indirect photographic stencils

This method is used commercially for very precise work, such as the reproduction of fine line drawings and medium half-tone screens. The diapositive is copied on to a light-sensitive pigment paper in a vacuum pressure frame. After exposure, this paper is immersed in cold water and pressed on to a smooth, temporary transfer support such as a sheet of waxed cellulose nitrate, or of polyester, etc. The plate is then soaked in warm water, the paper is peeled off and the soluble gelatine is washed away. The screen is now pressed in contact with the wet stencil which is supported on a glass plate. When everything is dry the temporary support can be pulled away cleanly.

Removing the stencil

You can remove the stencil from used screens. The technique varies with the type of stencil; the following is typical. First clean the screen thoroughly. Remove any hardened remnants of colour with a suitable solvent, and brush the screen with a nylon brush and a 10 per cent caustic soda solution. This removes the last traces of fat or oil. Rinse the screen well and then brush a potassium permanganate solution (1 part to 100 of water) on both sides of the screen with a nylon brush. You will see the screen coating turn brown as the solution attacks it. Now wash off the potassium permanganate and remove the coating by rubbing on potassium metabisulphite or sodium bisulphite powder with a stiff brush. Finally wash the screen with a 2 per cent sulphuric acid solution and rinse it well with water. After drying the screen is clean and ready for further use.

Printing ink

Prints can be made with linseed oil- or varnish-based colours or with special silk-screen inks, all available in a large range of colours. There are matt and gloss colours, bronze dusting powder and binder, and also fluorescent colours and dyes in the three standard colour-printing shades. The matt and gloss colours can be mixed at will and reduced in intensity by a "stretcher". This works like a thinner and has the same effect as adding water to water colours. The fluorescent colours can be mixed only with one another if their fluorescent effect is to be retained.

The printing dyes give subtractive colour mixing when overprinted, and can also be lightened and increased in quantity with a thinner. You can print with water-based colours without ill effects through screens coated with shellac or a photographic emulsion. For instance you can make up your own colour to print a solid, matt area. Take a decorator's powder colour, or better a much finer artist's powder colour, and mix it well. Take as much powder as you will need for the number of prints and soak it in a large container and leave for half an hour to an hour. You may add powder white to the colour to give it more body so that it will cover better. Lithophane white, zinc white, or titanium white are best for this. The water should come just above the top of the powder. Do not be too sparing when mixing the colour. A lot of colour remains in the screen and must be washed out unused after printing. Most colour is used at the first pass, as it fills the mesh of the gauze, so you will only be able to gauge the amount of colour you need after the second or third prints.

In the meantime mix a good supply of cellulose paste. This is a paste used by decorators for hanging wallpaper. Mix it according to the instructions on the packet. When the time is right, mix the water standing above the colour in with the paste in about 1 : 1 or 1 : 3 parts. To reduce the intensity of the colour even more, mix more cellulose paste with it. It is advisable in this case to mix one part of wheat starch, as the bookbinder uses, to each part of cellulose paste. This gives the colour the necessary pasty consistency for printing.

You can easily make transparent colours yourself by colouring the cellulose and starch mixture with aniline dyes to the right tone. Here you can use photographic glazing dyes as used for colouring prints, or the cheapest wood stains. Both these are aniline dyes, and you can obtain the latter in powder form. You can dissolve them in water and mix them with any colours on the same base. Ask for water-soluble aniline dye in the shop.

The disadvantage of printing with water colours is that it is difficult to avoid slight stretching and shrinking of the paper. The paper cockles after the first print and this leads to alignment difficulties with the second one. You can alleviate this by using heavier paper and by pressing the dry print under a glass plate for a few hours before printing the next colour. You can remove the waviness before printing by moistening the back of the paper with a slightly damp sponge, but protect the printed side with a porous sheet while you do this.

Apart from this tendency, especially of thin papers, to cockle when printed with water colours, all paper sorts are equally well suited for silk screen printing. The best sorts are drawing cards and good printing papers. To get pure colours it is advisable to use white-surfaced papers.

Preparing the screen

Choose a screen which is plenty big enough, so that the design does not extend right to the edges of the gauze. Mask the borders of the screen out with a paper mask and adhesive tape on both sides of the screen so that colour running round the edge of the squeegee will not drip through on to the print. This mask should be at least $1\frac{1}{4}$ in. (3 cm.) wide along the long sides and 2 in. (5 cm.) at the ends to provide a margin for the colour brought at each pass by the squeegee.

Before printing a long run with water colours, coat the masking strips at the sides with shellac. When you have corrected the last details with varnish fix the screen to the base plate. The screen frame has hinges which are adjustable in height. Set these so that the screen stands about $\frac{1}{8}$ in. (2–3 mm.) above the paper when it is lowered. Some more sophisticated screens have a device which automatically raises the screen after each print.

When printing with colour screens, it is advisable to stick two or three corner pieces on the base plate to locate the paper accurately. This ensures good alignment of the component colour prints provided the screens have been made from the same original.

Printing

Pour the thick ink into the end of the lowered screen and draw it lightly over the gauze with the squeegee, a hard rubber or plastic blade. The squeegee presses the screen down on to the paper for a brief instant as it passes and the ink flows through the open mesh on to the paper surface. The screen springs away again immediately the squeegee has passed, preventing an excess of ink reaching the paper. If the paper tends to rise and remain stuck to the screen correct this by thinning the ink a little. A good base plate is a sheet of hardboard coated with a slow-drying adhesive. After about half an hour, when the glue is half-dry, it will hold the paper wonderfully in place on the board.

In commercial screen printing works the paper is laid on a vacuum table. The table is covered with tiny holes leading to an exhaust pump, and the sheets are held by the air pressure above. Lay the finished prints on tables to dry or hang them on a line with clothes pegs. You can buy special drying hangers, which are even better.

Cleaning the screen

You must clean the screen very thoroughly after printing or the colour will remain in the mesh. Here it will harden and often be impossible to remove. You can obtain cleaning agents for all the normal silk-screen colours, but you can use cellulose thinners, or a solution of equal parts of benzine, xylol, and turpentine or even plain benzine to the same effect. Finally wash the screen with warm, soapy water. It is much easier to clean a screen after using water colours. All you need is a powerful jet of cold water from a tap or spray. This is perhaps the greatest advantage of using water colours.

Replacing the gauze

If the screen is worn out through use or has been accidentally damaged you can remove the gauze and replace it with new. There are various kinds of material available, sold by the yard from the roll. Natural silk gauze is best for cut-out stencils: nylon mesh would be damaged by the heat of the iron used for fixing the stencil. On the other hand nylon gauzes are very durable and elastic. They need careful stretching to prevent alignment errors. Nylon screens are suitable for glue stencils and both direct and indirect photographic methods. Lastly there are bronze and chrome-steel meshes. These gauzes are dimensionally stable but are at the same time very sensitive to impact damage. They can kink and give unclean prints. There are different grades of gauze, the most widely used having 250, 300, and 350 threads per inch.

Cut a piece of gauze to size about $\frac{3}{8}$ in. (1 cm.) larger all round than the outside dimensions of the frame. Stretch the material evenly over the frame, holding down the folded-over edges with staples, pins, or drawing-pins. Coat the area across the top of the frame with universal glue or adhesive varnish. After about 30 minutes drying time you can remove the pins and cut away the spare edges. The material gains its proper tautness when you screw this frame to the tensioning frame.

"Rainbow" prints

With some skill you can make "rainbow prints", with continuous colour changes with a silk screen. Pour the colour side by side in the strip at the end of the screen and mix the colours a little with a brush before using the squeegee. Draw the colours only once over the screen and you will have a rainbow print.

Natural material prints

There are several possible ways of making prints of natural materials.

Coat the gauze with a light-sensitive emulsion and lay the skeleton leaf, or cell structure, or whatever you wish to print on the screen. Weigh this down with a sheet of glass fitting inside the frame and expose in sunlight or in a copying machine. Take the usual precautions to prevent reflections from the back of the

Natural print from a skeleton leaf

screen. Of course you can use this method only with flat objects. If the objects seem a little too transparent, paint them with poster black before copying. The second method is to sensitize the screen in the usual way and to expose it in the sun until it hardens. Then soak the subject in potassium permanganate solution and press it carefully on to the screen. This decomposes the screen where it touches and you now wash out these areas with bisulphate solution or powder. To print three-dimensional objects like twigs, or fir cones you must first make photograms from them with photographic film and a strong point light. You can then copy this diapositive on to the screen in the normal way.

These are only a few of the almost inexhaustible possibilities offered by silk-screen printing. With imagination and patience you can make full use of this childishly simple yet highly developed process in the most varied fields. The ability to discover new applications and ways is a matter of experience, which you will rapidly gain by practising the technique.

TYPOGRAPHY

Stanley Morison defined typography as "the craft of rightly disposing printing material to suit a specific purpose; of so arranging the letters, distributing the space and controlling the type as to aid to the maximum the reader's comprehension of the text. . . . "

The distinguishing characteristic of good typography is the proper and considered distribution of matter on the paper. It is not so important to obtain the most perfectly formed types as to achieve good results with any types available. The type face must always be suitable to the subject matter in form and weight. One must however consider whether the type which harmonizes with the subject matter in style is also easily legible.

Aesthetic considerations may be secondary to practical considerations. When debating the virtues of one typeface against others, for advertising purposes, remember the tremendous and overruling importance of legibility. In poster work, for example, the restrained, but easily understandable, sans serif types are often preferable to other type families with more complicated letter forms. This is not to say that sans serif types have the edge on all others in the

Typesetting arrangements:
1 Symmetrical (lines of different lengths ranged about the centre line)
2 Asymmetrical (lines of different length ranged from the left)
3 Asymmetrical (lines of different length ranged from the right)
4 Justified (all lines the same length)

matter of legibility—in fact several of the classical book types are acknowledgedly very legible. The size of the letters plays a great role here. The classical faces tend to lose their clarity in the larger sizes, and must then concede ease of legibility to the sans serif faces.

In typography we differentiate between type layouts according to the way the lines are arranged. We talk of symmetrical and asymmetrical arrangements, and of solid setting.

Symmetrical setting

As its name suggests, this is a symmetrical distribution of the type about the centre-line of the page. Each line, regardless of its length, is centred symmetrically. This arrangement is widely used for book titles of works of fiction. It is also much used for hand-written or drawn book titles. This distribution is suitable for short texts. When longer texts are set, the many different lengths of line form a complicated pattern. This is confusing and makes it difficult to follow the text. The most important aim of any printing, whether poster, newspaper advertisement, or pamphlet, is to be easily legible and understandable. To achieve this, we must reduce the text to the minimum necessary, and arrange it clearly on the page.

Asymmetrical setting

An asymmetrical arrangement of typematter is often used for display and other forms of jobbing composition. Here, the lines of type are arranged toward the left of the page. This arrangement makes for easily legible texts and is very suitable for prospectuses, pamphlets, catalogues, etc. It is also widely used for poster work and newspaper announcements. In these cases the uneven length of line is a help in separating the ideas for the reader, making the matter easy to read.

Asymmetrical setting makes the compositor's work much easier because he does not have to justify each line.

With the asymmetrical arrangement it is possible to displace parts of the text. In many cases it is a great help to use the centre-line as a starting point for the lines of text, the lines beginning at the centre of the page and running from left ro right as usual. This method is especially useful when the text contains many short paragraphs and titles or requires many hanging notes. The titles or notes can be started as usual at the left of the page, and thus stand out well from the normal text. Paragraph and section titles may be set in bold type to further guide the eye and to give a clearer overall picture.

Other suitable starting points are at a third and two-thirds of the way across the page. In the same way the page may be divided by the "golden section" or for special purposes at any aesthetically suitable point.

Solid setting

Newspapers, magazines and books are usually printed with "justified" lines; that is to say they are all of equal length, and both the left-hand and right-hand margins are even. The lines are justified by the insertion of spaces between the words (word spacing), or in some cases between individual letters (letter spacing). In hand composition the compositor fills out the line with uniform spacing as far as possible, and when there is a word too long for the line, he has to decide whether it can be split and hyphenated, or carried to the next line. In machine composition, justification is semi-automatic, but the keyboard operator still has to make similar decisions.

The question whether the traditional rectangular form of text composition is ideal has been much debated in recent years. Lines of unequal length can be set more economically than justified lines, and this is a question of some importance in computer typesetting. There is no special difficulty about justification with a computer, so long as there are only few restrictions as to where words should be split and hyphenated. Many systems are now available for partial solution of the problem, but to produce completely acceptable text it would be necessary to provide the computer with a fairly large dictionary store of words, and this would add appreciably to the already high cost. So far there is little evidence to show that asymmetrical text setting would be generally acceptable to authors, publishers and the reading public, and it seems that rectangular composition will continue at the expense of slightly imperfect hyphenation.

Asymmetrical setting is however often used for typewriter composition. Good repro proofs are made on an ordinary typewriter in the production of photo-litho plates for offset printing. The work is aligned at the left-hand margin, but the lines are of unequal length. This is an economical form of production for short editions of reports, scientific papers, and other work which otherwise might not be published.

Classifications of composition

Three main types of composition are classified today: jobbing composition, display work, and solid setting. Jobbing composition is the setting of work by hand to an individual design or sketch. A wide range of type-faces and sizes is available to the jobbing compositor, and he also makes use of printers' flowers, lines, and other decorative elements. Jobbing composition is used for posters, advertisements, stationery, pro-grammes, diplomas and so on, the work being carried out exactly to the designer's wishes. The compositor must have long experience and a feel for the work, and usually charges more for this type of work than for more routine jobs. Solid or text composition is done mainly on a typesetting machine. The type normally used ranges from 8–12 pt. Machine setting is used for all book and magazine texts.

News composition is now done entirely on machines, only the titles being set by hand or on the Ludlow cast-ing machine and added later. This, of course, is only a broad classification. The three methods can never be entirely separated: there will always be borderline cases where perhaps two methods are used together.

However, as a broad classification of the methods used in book, magazine, newspaper, and display work, the division must stand.

Posters

Their bold scale and unlimited possibilities make posters one of the most interesting design problems. Posters represent perhaps the summit of advertising, and also have an educational duty in presenting the public with good aesthetic standards. The main duty of a poster is to be conspicuous, to pack a punch. This is achieved by lively colouring, or by use of an unusual photograph, or by some characteristic symbol. This can be anything from realistic to humorous, or be directly grotesque.

At all costs the poster on the hoarding or bus-side must awake the interest of passers-by at a distance. They will then take the trouble to find out what it is all about by a closer examination of the attached text.

If it accomplishes this, the poster is already a success as an advertising medium.

When designing a poster, remember to ensure that the main text is legible at a distance. For this the letters must stand out against the coloured or neutral background of the poster and must be set in a size in proportion to the area of the poster. The lettering must be separated from the main picture of the poster yet remain integrated with the whole. This interdependence must not be subdued: the lettering and picture must combine to form a graphic unity. Remember to specify only fast and waterproof colours for poster printing. If you do not, sun and weather will soon play havoc with your work: the colours will fade and run.

Errata slips

Errata slips are small printed labels stuck over parts of a poster. They are used when certain details (dates, prices, or times) have been altered in the meantime. Take care that these slips are the same colour as the poster background, so that they do not disturb the overall balance.

Advertisements

A well-designed, dignified advertisement will always have distinction and be noticed among others striving after effect. As with a poster, the placing of the wording is important, in order to achieve some separation from the surrounding advertisements. Do not try simply to fill the space to the edges, but try rather to concentrate the lettering more at the centre, leaving free space on all sides. You can achieve the effect by using only a short text and leaving much white paper space. If necessary, see if it is possible to still further reduce the text.

In general, there are many possibilities open in advertisement design: bold headlines, mixtures of different types and sizes, white letters on black, and cut-outs of all possible shapes; these are all legitimate, and doubtless have a very powerful effect, but they cannot really claim to be essential to good advertising.

A certain antidote to this obtrusiveness is to use a simple form and the minimum number of elements necessary to obtain the desired effect. The best advertisement should communicate with the consumer whose interest is to be aroused. This communication should be concise and informative to bring the reader to the point of the matter as quickly and simply as possible. Interest can be aroused by a photograph or drawing, in black-and-white or colour. It must be pertinent to the text, and you should take pains that the two do not contradict one another.

Poster and advertisement layout

Restrictions of paper size and type size, and considerations of column width in magazines and catalogues do not allow of an arbitrary arrangement of text and illustrations. A general layout of type area and illustrations can be prepared for a paper of a particular size, to be used as basis for posters, advertisements and catalogues and so on. This layout cannot claim to be the only correct solution in a particular case, but it will fulfil its purpose by ensuring good legibility thanks to its businesslike and restrained design.

We will take the design of a purely typographic poster as an example: the poster will be one of the standard sizes. Non-standard sizes are used only in very special cases, as all the wasted paper trimmed off by the printer is charged to the customer, and this effectively makes the poster dearer. When the size of the poster is known, a legible type can be chosen. The size of the type should be in a reasonable proportion to the size of the sheet, and must be legible from a distance. In most cases a clear-cut sans serif type is suitable.

Posters are often set in lower case letters alone. This gives clear blocks of text of even appearance, but a combination of upper and lower case is much more legible.

There are always certain words or lines in a poster or advertisement which must dominate the rest of the text. Set important words in larger or heavier type, and set accompanying text smaller, half the size being best.

Commission a printer to set the text solid in the required types and send you as many proofs as you need. Most printers have their own composing department and it is thus advisable to commission the same printer to do both the setting and the subsequent printing. When you receive the proofs from the printer, your first job is to compose a suitable layout with the set text, cutting it up as necessary to the right format. The design of the layout must be your own concern, but there are one or two general rules.

1. To prevent the text drifting off and looking as if it belongs to the neighbouring poster, it should be rather concentrated towards the centre. This will separate the whole poster from surrounding matter on the hoarding. Arrange the individual lines to give a compact and unified block of text.
2. The lines of text must be sensibly distributed. If the paper is not wide enough to allow the lines to be set completely they must be divided suitably. Try at all costs to avoid splitting words.
3. The text should be organized into groups of related ideas, and headings and paragraphs should be separated from one another. Separate headings can be emphasized by leaving sufficient space between them and the text. Accompanying text can be divided into clearly recognizable paragraphs by using blank lines.

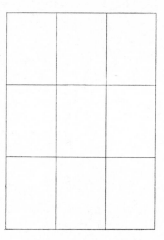

A poster sheet divided into thirds by guide lines

4. It is very helpful to divide the sheet as you wish with light pencil lines. This makes the composition much easier.
5. With an asymmetrical composition, it is advisable to range the lines of type from the left, so that the first letters of each line are directly under one another. This arrangement is most conducive to quick reading, since the eye is accustomed to seeking the beginning of a line at the left.
6. With symmetrical arrangements, range the lines from the middle, using the pencilled lines as a guide.
7. As far as the text allows, set heading lines in the top half or third of the paper, and the remaining text underneath after a large space. Place any lines appearing

above the heading well up towards the top of the paper.

8. When the lines are set roughly in place, they must be adjusted accurately. For this you will need a type measure, a ruler scaled in points or ems. It is advisable to work out a scheme of spacing based on divisions or multiplications of a definite unit of points or ems. This unit may be arbitrary, but should not be derived directly from the type size, as this results in awkward spacing when the unit is doubled, causing an optical break-up of the type area. It is best to base the proportion of the spacing unit to type size on the "golden section." Let us take as an example a poster with two sizes of type, one of 5 pica (56 pt), and the smaller of 2·5 pica (28 pt). The golden section ratio of 1 : 1·6 gives us a ratio of type size to space of 5 : 8. This means the spacing unit is 8 ems.

Now the text can be set in position and fixed in place. From the basic unit of 8 ems we can get spaces of 16 and 24 ems by doubling and tripling. Assuming that 24 ems is about the right distance from the heading to the first line of text, mark the place with a light pencil line and set the first line of text in place. The line spacing in the blocks of accompanying text can also be calculated according to the golden section. With a 28 pt type the space unit will be 45 pt ($28 : x = 1 : 1·6$). You can also fix the width of the left-hand margin in the same way. Still using our example, the margin could be 8, 16, or 24 ems. If using the golden section makes the spaces too wide in proportion to the size of type, reduce the proportion to 1 : 1·4 or 1 : 1·2. This should not be reduced much further, as the spaces between lines of solid set type will no longer be distinct.

Using a scheme as described here does not mean that the same proportions and sizes must be used for all the blocks of text and their spaces. The design can be made stimulating by a skilful variation of the basic unit of points or ems. Only where a poster or printed sheet contains complete and independent paragraphs each with its own heading can all the spaces be made even (for instance in programmes).

Above all you must consider the legibility of the poster and its resulting informative value. To ensure that the type does not appear to be slipping out of the bottom of the design, set the heading in a larger or heavier type. If possible it should be in the top half of the sheet, with its first line not below the centre line of the page.

Distribution of type on a photographic
poster. The lines were arranged on
a plan dividing the sheet vertically into
thirds. The horizontal placing was determined by the picture

The system just described will be a great help for all kinds of work where type must be arranged to a given format. The way the system is put to use remains the concern of the designer. In the long run the determining factor in typographic design is a sure feeling for the relationship of the type to the surrounding area.

9. When the layout planning is finished, attach the set lines to the paper and write dimensions on the sheet. Take the measurements from base line to base line and insert the dimensions in the margin in units of points or ems. Write any notes necessary for the printing in the margins in the corresponding place—e.g. "red type on white ground", "black type on yellow paper" or "negative type on blue ground", and so on. The last named is suitable for offset litho printing. Only a small increase in cost is involved, as it is easy to copy the original directly on to a negative. A colour sample should be included with the layout to help the printer to reproduce the design accurately.

10. Deliver the finished layout to the printer.

Catalogues and advertising leaflets

The aspects of typography and illustration mentioned so far apply to the design of catalogues, books, and magazines in general. However, the illustration of catalogues and advertising leaflets plays a critical part and merits great attention. Two things are especially important: the matter should be original, and command attention through its form, colour, illustration, and wording. The information contained should be to the point and clearly expressed: the reader must be led at once to the heart of the matter.

A great interest has been shown in standardizing the size of such literature, and the British Standards Institution recommends the use of the ISO "A" sizes A4 and A5 $8\frac{1}{4} \times 11\frac{1}{4}$ in. (210×297 mm.) and $5\frac{7}{8} \times 8\frac{1}{4}$ in. (148×210 mm.). Different foldings may be used to achieve interesting variations, such as $\frac{1}{3}$ A4 vertical or horizontal. Almost square pages are obtained by using $\frac{2}{3}$ A4 or $\frac{2}{3}$ A3 sized sheets. Leaflets are often folded concertina fashion, and catalogues are usually inset and stapled.

The choice of illustrations is especially critical. Choose only the best pictures for printing: it is better to discard a mediocre or bad picture or to substitute a better one than to ruin the work with it.

An asymmetrical text arrangement is especially well suited to advertising leaflets: it brings a dynamic, essential character to the text. Instinctively the text can be formed into short, punchy lines. The size and face of the type will depend on the length of the text and the number of sides available, and also on the intended character of the work.

Do not choose too small a type. This is difficult to read, and will therefore not be read. On the other hand, do not use too large a type. This can have a vulgar appearance which can be just as damaging in the end.

The proportions of type, illustration, and empty paper must be right. Each individual part, as well as the whole must function well.

Newspapers

As there are more than 400 newspapers in Britain, there are many different sizes, as you would expect. There are no standard sizes, but the sizes fall into two main categories:
Broadsheet 16 × 24 in.
Tabloid 12 × 14½ in.
The newspaper size depends on the width and circumference of the printing rollers used. Newspapers also use a wide variety of machine-set types, but perhaps most use an 8 pt condensed face set in several columns, normally six to eight. The type for newspaper work must be easily legible and must not contain exceptionally fine lines and serifs, which would make stereotyping difficult. The newspaper must be so designed that it appears lively and interesting while retaining its character.

The headlines complete the typographic picture and direct attention to the articles. They should be placed as far as possible in the same position in each edition for ease of quick reading. Restrict yourself to only a few different sizes and faces of type for newspaper design in the interests of clarity. Headlines must not merge together visually, even when they are side by side above neighbouring articles.

The size of illustrations depends on the column width. They may be printed from half-tone or line blocks. Originals for half-tone blocks must have good contrasts. Definition of the finer tones is reduced during the block making, and many more tones are lost in the printing.

A half-page advertisement. The area
has the same height and width as a
column of type

A two-thirds page advertisement with
cut-out pictures

Citroën 2CV

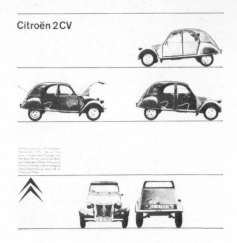

Newspapers are made up on pre-printed make-up
sheets showing the columns. The headlines and illustrations are pasted up on to these sheets. When the
main text has been made up, the other parts such as
local news, theatre programmes, and advertisements
are filled in as and where possible.

Magazine cover design

It is difficult to find a universal form for a magazine
cover giving the desired character and at the same time
being impressive. There are many types of magazine:
weeklies, local news magazines, trade journals, church
and society magazines, and so on.

These cover many different fields in as many different styles. Whereas the news magazines and trade
journals are mainly concerned with factual reporting
of events or developments in their fields, the weeklies
and picture magazines thrive more on sensation and
striking presentation. Such magazines are stimulating
from the design point of view. They are recognized by
their bright covers and bold type.

There are many ways of designing a cover title. The
type may be related to that of the text or it may form a
direct contrast. It may be the same face as the text,
but larger or bold or extra bold; it may be of an entirely
different family or even hand-drawn. When a contrast
is wanted, you may use a square title and round text
type or vice-versa, or use serif and sans serif against
one another.

Sketching typefaces

Typographic designs can be prepared in sketch form; with practice you will be able to sketch type of all sorts and sizes accurately and convincingly. Obtain sample sheets of type faces from the printer and use these as models to copy from. Take a sheet with the right type face and size and measure off the capital and x-height of the letters. Transfer these measurements to your paper and draw parallel guide lines to help with the drawing. Use a soft pencil, about B, for bold type, a medium (H or HB) for normal type and a hard one (2–3H) for thin letters. Copy the letters as accurately as you can. It is most important that the width of the letters and the spacing is correct if you are to be able to judge the length of the set lines.

Sketched letters

Printed letters

Smaller type sizes forming an area of type with several lines are sketched in exactly the same way, but here the type measure and the leading of the lines must be taken into account. Use a line gauge, a ruler with measurements in points and ems, to lay out the type area accurately.

If you have already contracted a printer to print your design it is better to enter directly into agreement with him in this matter. Choose your type from trial pulls at the printer's and let him set the text and supply a number of pulls.

Now, cutting these pulls as required you can group the words and lines as you wish and stick them down in position on the plan of the type area which you have drawn. The printer will later set and print the type as you have shown it in this layout.

Announcements

Private and business announcements in newspapers are usually printed on specially reserved pages and can have a width of one, two, or more columns. The advertisement pages should have a uniform appearance and the various groups should be clearly headed.

Well-designed announcements should be set in a legible type and should not contain more than two or three different sizes of type. As long as the announcement achieves clarity by good setting of the headings and text, it can be considered well designed. The various section headings "Situations Vacant", "For Sale", "Wanted", and so on, are used in every edition of a newspaper, and for this reason are usually held in the form of type-high stereo blocks.

A page of advertisements in an Argentine newspaper published in 1838. The titles are marked by symbolic vignettes

The front page of THE TIMES was
traditionally given over to advertisements
until 1965

A margin or line is usually printed between advertisements to separate them from one another. The margin between neighbouring columns is usually equal to one or two times the measure of the typeface. Each advertisement can be separated arbitrarily from the next by setting blank lines. Announcements are sometimes framed with a thin line to isolate them from their surroundings.

Commercial advertisements

Manufacturing companies use space in newspapers, magazines, and sometimes even in books, to advertise their services or products. The greater part of the production costs of a publication can be paid by the fees for such advertisements. So it is that magazines with few or no advertisements are generally dearer than their counterparts with more. On the other hand, the firm who advertises expects to profit from the advertisement as well. You see again that it is important that the advertisement be forceful to achieve its end.

The size of the advertisement depends on the proportions of the magazine page, and generally of the width of the columns. We speak of 1/1, 1/2, 1/4, 1/8, 1/16 advertisements. These fractions do not refer to the linear size of the advertisement, but are a relation of its area to that of the page. For instance, a 1/4 ad. may take up the top fourth of the page, be almost square, or be a long strip along one side. The cost of the space is related to the cost of the whole page in the same way. Thus the manufacturer and designer can choose many forms for a given size and price.

Newspaper display advertisements can take various shapes and sizes. The sizes shown here vary from $\frac{1}{2}$ to $\frac{1}{32}$ page

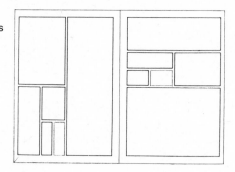

Try to avoid designing newspaper advertisements with fine line drawings or diagrams. Newspapers are printed on rotary printing machines using curved stereos. Very fine lines may break away as the mould for the stereo is bent to the right curvature and will not show on the final print.

Commercial advertisements often appear simultaneously or successively in several publications. For this reason it is not possible to use a typeface which will harmonize equally well with that of each individual publication. It is better to use a clear, neutral typeface with a simple character. Compose the text and slogans or headlines sensibly and distribute the whole well in relation to the space available. Asymmetrical, rather than symmetrical setting is to be recommended for longer texts. The various advertising points to be stressed generally are of uneven length and this justifies the use of asymmetrical setting.

The size of photographs and drawings used will depend on the size of the text and the space. Technical products may be depicted without a background. However, when you are showing more than one product, make sure that the photographs are all to the same scale. Here again the text should not fill the space too completely. The optical separation of the advertisement from its surroundings can be achieved simply by leaving white space all around, or by framing the space with lines.

An advertisement or series must often be planned so that it can be reproduced in colour or in black and white without changing its character. This factor is of great importance for the design when the advertisement is to be widely disseminated. Very few magazines print with a second colour, and when they do, this always seems to be the one colour not in your design. You will thus seldom be able to base your designs principally on the coloured conception. You will more often have to base your ideas on the black-and-white appearance of the design and hope that it will be possible to introduce a second or third colour or perhaps later to produce four-colour blocks. Just as the poster shouts from its hoarding or bus-side, the advertisement must command attention in the middle of its newspaper. This can be achieved only by limiting the elements to the essentials. Do not fall into the habit of using the same design solution for all problems. Suit your design to the requirements, now using restrained technical motives, and now literary, humorous, or fanciful solutions.

Letterheads

General rules for the design of letterheads are given by the British Standards Institution (BS 1808 : 1963). Postal regulations, the related size of envelopes and the use of window or aperture envelopes have made it necessary to recommend standard sizes of paper. The wide range previously in use has been reduced to the following sizes:

8 × 10 in. (203 × 254 mm.).
5 × 8 in. (127 × 203 mm.).

During the last few years the A4 and A5 sizes from the A-range recommended by the International Standards Organization (ISO) in their Recommendation R216 have gained considerable popularity.
ISO-size

A4 $8\frac{1}{4}$ × $11\frac{3}{4}$ in. (210 × 297 mm.).
A5 $5\frac{7}{8}$ × $8\frac{1}{4}$ in. (148 × 210 mm.).

Design

First you must make a rough layout of the sheet. The best way to start is by dividing the sheet horizontally and vertically into a number of fields. These divisions enable you to distribute the lettering more clearly. Choose a clear, legible type which will harmonize well with the writing to be used on the paper. The size of the various fields will depend on the purpose of the paper and on the type of writing, typewriter or hand-writing, to be used. If the paper is to be used in a typewriter, the machine impressions must of course line up with the printed lines. The distance between single-spaced typewritten lines is $\frac{1}{6}$ in. (approx. 4·2 mm.). It is a great help to run a sheet of tracing paper the same size as the letter paper through the typewriter and to type a line along the top and down the left-hand side using only capital X. Use single spacing for the vertical row.

The letterhead should be clear and forceful. The title, or company name, adress, telephone number, list of directors and other similar information should be so placed that they are not obscured when the letter is filed with others.

You should leave a clear margin for filing clips, etc.,

at least 1 in. (25·4 mm.) at the left of the paper before the first typed letter. This is equivalent to 10 typewriter impressions.

The layout must show limiting marks for the address area. The size and position of this area is related to the window or aperture in the envelopes (see aperture envelopes).

There must generally be much more space for references on commercial forms than on business letter paper. Try to keep to as few as possible in the layout. The references are in the following order: Date, Your ref., Our ref.

The distance between lines of single-spaced type-written matter is $\frac{1}{6}$ in. (4·2 mm. approx.). The distance between horizontal rulings must thus be multiples of this distance, so that the lines can be typed on the machine.

Commercial forms

The following are some of the commercial forms you may meet: purchase orders, packaging notes, despatch notes, delivery notes, invoices, statements of account.

These forms are in effect an extended variety of normal letterheads. To maintain a family likeness, use the same letterhead as on the writing paper, complete with address area. On the purchase order form the buyer's delivery address stands left, next to the supplier's address. On invoices, despatch notes and packaging notes the consignee's area is in the top third of the sheet. If the entry in the consignee's area is the same as that in the addressee's area, the name and address should be entered only in the latter.

There are many ways of giving references. When they spread across the whole width of the form they should be in the following order: Customer's ref., Supplier's ref., Date.

Leave space for instructions under the references. These instructions will vary from form to form. Note clearly what is to be entered: e.g. Delivery date, Method of transit, etc.

The body of the form should be left clear for the particular purpose, and this should be clearly stated: description of goods, quantity, price, amount, etc. Monetary forms should be divided into columns with fine lines. When invoices are to be rendered in £. s. d., do not rule vertical lines in the "amounts" column.

A width of 2·4 in. (60–96 mm.) has been found suitable for the "price per" and "amounts" columns.

It is generally impossible for a machine to type right to the bottom of the page. You can use this space for further instructions or other information such as warranties or statutory notices, buyer's certification for payment, terms of payment, etc. If these notes are lengthy it may be better to print them on the back of the form and include a footnote to this effect. As with letter paper, the printing on these forms must be placed to line up with the lines of typewriting.

Envelopes

Post Office regulations provide that envelopes must not be less than 4 in. (10·1 cm.) in length or $2\frac{3}{4}$ in. (7cm.) in width. They should preferably be white, but may also be a pale shade of beige, yellow, green, or blue. Red, or wholly transparent envelopes are not allowed. The right-hand half of the address side should be reserved exclusively for the addressee's name and address and a space of at least $1\frac{1}{2}$ in. (3·8 cm.) should be left free for the stamps and postmarks.

The panel must extend parallel to the length of the envelope. At least $1\frac{1}{2}$ in. (3·8 cm.) must be left above the window for the stamps and postmarks. No writing or printing other than the addressee's name and address should appear through the panel.

The cut-out aperture or window must not be larger than $3\frac{3}{4}$ in. (9·5 cm.) in length or $1\frac{1}{4}$ in. (3·1 cm.) wide, and there must be at least $\frac{1}{2}$ in. (12 mm.) between the cut-out panel and the sides of the envelope. The enclosure must be so folded that it cannot move and cause the name and address to be hidden. Aperture envelopes are inadmissible in the International Service.

Business cards

Business cards are used by representatives and executives, and must present information about the business concern, its name, branch, and address. They may also carry a list of articles or services produced or offered, and the name of the bearer.

A firm's business cards are its heralds and must be designed to leave the client with a good impression of the quality and ideals of the firm. The choice of layout, whether asymmetrical or symmetrical, and the typeface is up to you as the designer. The size of type you use will depend on the size of the card and the amount of text to be printed. It is essential to organize the type into clear groups and to strike a good balance between the type area and the card size.

Visiting cards

Visiting cards are printed on stiff white paper or card using the simplest typographic means. The card should be so designed that the profession and status of the bearer are readily apparent. You will obtain the best results by using type sparingly on a white ground: the type should not appear too obtrusive.

Take a type between 8 and 12 pt for the name and a smaller type of 5–8 pt for the address. The exact size of the type for the address will depend on the number of syllables in the address. In the best cases you will be able to use the same size of type for the name and address. Choose a suitable, restrained type. You can get attractive results by printing this in grey or another colour. Leave out decorative elements or the card will grow into a brash, arty sales ticket.

Greetings cards

These may be congratulatory cards for births, christenings, engagements, marriages, or a host of other occasions. Apart from a few general restrictions in size, you can really let your imagination go on the design of these cards: you can produce restrained typographic designs or jolly hand-drawn or photographic solutions.

The card must be friendly and appealing and have a clear message. There are so many ways of producing an engaging result that the field is always interesting. You can also develop new methods of folding, so that the card may be sent folded or may be erected to form a solid unit later. You may even think of stamping the card into several parts to be put together like a puzzle. By folding a sheet twice at right-angles you can print the whole sheet in one operation and have text or illustrations both outside and inside.

Christmas and New Year cards

It is a pleasant custom to send friends, business aquaintances, and relations best wishes in the form of a card. However, it is a mistake to regard this as a tiresome duty and consequently simply to buy some of the many badly-designed and tasteless cards available

113

in the shops. You will give much more satisfaction and receive much more respect by sending an original card, with an appropriate theme and a good design. You may care to include a vignette or geometrical symbol in one or more colours to introduce a valuable personal note which you will never find in a bought card. The exact size and form of the card and the paper quality remain free, but a colour printing will not be economical for the usual short run.

Obituary announcements

Keep such announcements as plain and simple as possible, and avoid all devices like palm leaves, wreaths, and so on. You will generally be able to obtain ready-printed envelopes with a black border for obituary notices. As far as possible print the paper and envelope with a narrow border and a small size of roman type. You may emphasize the name of the deceased in a bolder type to differentiate it from the other text. Set the names of the mourners in a normal or light type well placed in a block lower on the sheet. Set all the notices referring to funeral arrangements at the foot of the page in the same or an even smaller type.

Programmes

Programmes may be single sheets, printed on one or both sides, folded sheets, or bound booklets. The arrangement of the text of the programme depends on the type and title of the function, the names of the people appearing, and the nature of the events or functions. The programme must also show the name of the producer, the place and time of the events, and perhaps details of the admission ticket sales and booking. Try to complete your design with as few different types and type sizes as you can. For musical performances you may range the names of the composer and player from one side or set them in a block. This decision will depend on the setting of the remaining text, which may be asymmetrical or symmetrical.

Deeds and diplomas

These documents are usually printed singly and must have a dignified appearance. You can achieve this only by producing a well-considered, balanced, and timeless design. The very fact that only a single example of the document is printed, increases its value. To ensure this, choose a paper of the highest quality: use a genuine wood-free paper, not imitation parchment or mould-made paper. With regard to typography, a timeless symmetrical arrangement, with a sense of balance, is generally more suitable than an asymmetrical setting. However, it is equally possible that a well ordered asymmetrical arrangement could lead to an equally successful solution.

In the long run, the degree of distinction bestowed by the document must dictate the final design. As already said, a symmetrical setting demands a considered, balanced design. You must choose a type to do justice to the occasion, be it a jubilee or any other ceremonial gathering. The document may be a single sheet or may be folded and presented in a folder.

Legibility of type

The main purpose of type in printed or written form is to convey information. Disregarding the ornamental use of type, printed text is intended to be read easily and without strain. It has been found that the legibility of a certain typeface is high when it is possible to read a text with the lower half of the characters obscured. This indicates that the legibility of a type depends on the form variations of the ascenders of the lower case letters. Text composed from capitals only is notoriously difficult to read. It has been found that sans serifs and types like Times Roman and Bodoni are easily read. The type size used for setting has an influence on the readability of a column of text. Material to be read by grown-ups is advantageously composed in 10 point and for children in 12 to 14 points. Very small type, long lines, and paragraphs without sufficient leading between the lines are tiring to the eyes.

Reading is a recognition of words in the form of familiar letter groupings. The word picture creates the meaning in the brain, which explains why misspellings are only noticed when the familiar word image is disturbed.

BOOK DESIGN

The book starts with the manuscript. Manuscripts should be written on 13×8 in., 10×8 in., or ISO A4 paper, and the sheets should be numbered in sequence to ease the compositor's work. Heavily corrected manuscripts are difficult to read and lead to mis-understandings and composition errors. Isolated corrections may be made in the text. The standard correction marks (see page 127) are for use on printed proofs and should always be indicated in the margin. This is pointless in manuscripts, since the compositor is obliged to read the whole text in order to set it. You should indicate in the manuscript which parts of the text are to be set in capitals, heavy type, or italics for emphasis. You can do this by underlining the specific words, and repeating this sign in the margin with an explanatory note (caps, bold, or italics). When this comes repeatedly, it is enough to repeat the note only at the beginning of the text or once on each page. When you have clearly noted the typeface and size and all titles and chapter headings, you may deliver the manuscript to the printer. Before beginning the planning of a solid-set text, you must calculate how many printed sides the manuscript will produce. It is possible to produce a thick book from a short manuscript by using a suitable paper and leading the text heavily. You can also achieve the opposite by setting the text solid with narrow margins. Exact calculations can be made to estimate the amount of text and the number of sides the manuscript will produce (see page 125).

Specimen pages and dummy

It is advisable for any sizable printing job to commission tenders for the work from a number of printers. The tender offering the best quality work for the price will be the best one to choose. You must give the tendering printers full information on the character of the work, the number of sides, the type sort and the kind of setting, the type of paper, the book size, the binding, and the number of copies.

When the client has agreed one tender, you should order a specimen page printed to your design and also a dummy. A dummy is a sample copy of the work made up with the actual papers chosen, cut to the right size and bulk, and bound as you intend the book to be.

The typographic possibilities are many, and you will need full realization of them to solve the problems satisfactorily. Everything which can be said in this matter can only be a general guide. It is a different matter with the make-up of the text of the book. Here you must adhere to a constant type area.

Symmetrical type area

A symmetrical type area, the classic composition, as its name suggests, is the same on both sides. With this arrangement, the two outside margins of an opening (two facing pages) are each wider than the central margin, giving the whole spread a visual unity. The bottom margin is also wider than the top margin, firstly for aesthetic reasons, to counteract the tendency of the text to appear low on the page, and secondly to provide adequate space for the pagination. The printer has special names for the different margins:

top margin: head.   lower margin: tail.
outer margin: fore-edge.   inner margin: back.

In the classical arrangement the widths of the margins are related to one another in a definite proportion.

Back   head   fore-edge   tail
2   :   3   :   4   :   5

This gives a proportion of type area to page area of 5 : 8—the golden mean. This proportion can easily be

Classical positioning of a symmetrical type area. An arrangement according to the golden section is obtained by drawing in the diagonals of the single and double sheets

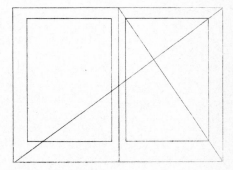

An opening with symmetrical type areas
and wide back margins. The top and outside
margins are the same width, as are
the bottom and inside margins

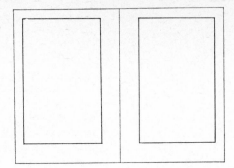

determined, on the golden mean principle, by dividing
each single page once diagonally and then dividing the
opening diagonally.

When using a symmetrical type area, it is in no way
essential to arrange the margins on the golden section principle. True, using this old printer's rule will
never do any harm, but in the long run it is an instinc-
tive feeling for good proportion, which again depends
on the size of paper, the number of lines, and the typeface which will decide. Stick to the rules just enough so
that the inner margins do not become too small and
allow the type to run together optically. In fact the
combined centre margin may well be wider than each
of the outer margins.

Asymmetrical type area

You may consciously distort the symmetry of the page
by moving the whole type area to the right of each page.
As it is a habit in the Western civilizations to read from
left to right, the reader will intuitively be led to the text
on the right-hand page and its verso.

An asymmetrical type area prevents each opening
being a fixed formal unit without progression. This
arrangement is disadvantageous in that the two type
areas on each side of a leaf do not coincide any longer
and it can happen that the reverse side shows through
a thin paper. This feature may also be reinforced by
"pressure". By this the printer means a slight embossing of the letters on the paper caused by excess
pressure in the press. This shows through the paper

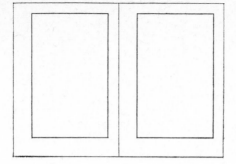

Asymmetrical type area arrangement.
Both blocks are displaced to the right,
giving inside margins of uneven width

and has a disturbing effect. It can be eliminated by choosing a suitable paper and printing very carefully.

Book types

When designing a book you must always choose a type sympathetic to the content of the book. The whole appearance and effect, and thus the commercial success of the book, depend to a great extent on the choice of type. For instance clear, restrained Grotesque or sans serif types are suitable for technical literature, whereas a fictional or romantic work is better printed in a good roman type. When you are in doubt as to which type to use, you should order specimen pages in different types and compare the intellectual and formal effect of each with the import of the text.

Book sizes

The following dimensions are for pages of books before trimming and are the sizes most commonly used for books in Great Britain.

Name	Size in inches of untrimmed page of book	mm.
Foolscap octavo	$4\frac{1}{4} \times 6\frac{3}{4}$	107×171
Crown octavo	$5 \times 7\frac{1}{2}$	127×190
Demy octavo	$5\frac{5}{8} \times 8\frac{3}{4}$	142×222
Medium octavo	$5\frac{3}{4} \times 9$	146×228
Royal octavo	$6\frac{1}{4} \times 10$	158×254
Crown quarto	$7\frac{1}{2} \times 10$	190×254
Demy quarto	$8\frac{3}{4} \times 11\frac{1}{4}$	222×285
Royal quarto	$10 \times 12\frac{1}{2}$	254×316

Indents and flush beginnings

One of the first tasks when designing a book is to decide on the form of the text setting. New paragraphs may be just as well indicated by an indent or a flush beginning. A flush beginning is admissible when the last line of the previous paragraph ends short of the last third of the line width. If, as sometimes happens, the last line occupies the full width, the next paragraph must be indented. You must decide right at the outset which method to use. You cannot combine the two. If you are using flush beginnings and the last line of the paragraph occupies the whole width, you must delete one or two unimportant words to reduce the length of the line. After you have chosen the sort of type and the size, you must design the type area plan, and hold rigidly to this through to the last page of the book.

The type area plan fixes the number of lines to a page, the length of the lines, and the setting arrangement of each page.

Pagination

Pagination is the numbering of each page in the book. The position of this number, or folio, as it is sometimes called, should be considered when designing the type area. It is practical to put the numbers on the left-hand pages in the bottom left-hand corner, and those on the right-hand pages in the bottom right, in each case with a blank line between number and text. This makes it easier and quicker to find any given side in the book.

Preliminary pages

Preliminary pages ("prelims") are the first pages of a book, containing all the matter preceding the main text. The prelims, together with the case, determine the outward character of the book, and their design should be considered in relation to the rest of the work The prelims are almost always printed after the rest of the book. They contain among other things the Contents page and List of Illustrations which can be compiled only when the pagination is finished. Most books have about eight pages of prelims, but more comprehensive works may have up to sixteen. Text pages are paginated with arabic numerals, whilst roman numerals are used for the prelims. Thus the text can be printed and paginated while the prelims are

The preliminary pages:
1 Half-title
2 Blank
3 Title
4 History of book and imprint
5 Dedication
6 Acknowledgements
7 Contents
8 List of illustrations or abbreviations

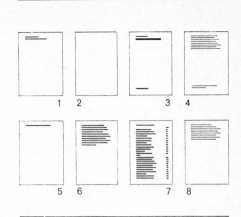

being compiled and set. The prelims are normally made up as follows:
Half-title
Title
History of book, imprint
Dedication
Acknowledgement
Contents
List of Illustrations
List of Abbreviations
Preface
Introduction

Half-title

The half-title is the first page of the book and protects the title-page from dirt. It usually contains simply the title of the book and the name of the author. The half-title along with the other prelims, should be visually integrated with the main body of the text. Set the title in the same typeface as the text on the first line of the type area decided on for the pages. There should be enough space between the book title and the author's name for them both to be clearly read. If the chapter headings of the text are centred on the middle of the page, this will of course have a bearing on the appearance of all the prelims. They must then be set symmetrically in the middle of the page too. An asymmetrical setting affords many more possibilities.

Frontispiece

The reverse, or verso, side of the half-title is usually left blank. If previous works by the same author, or other books of a series are to be mentioned, these are set on this page. Sometimes, a portrait of the author or an introductory illustration is wanted. This is printed on the verso of the half-title and is called the frontispiece. If a caption to the frontispiece is needed, set this in the same typeface as the text on the last line allowed by the type area chosen.

Title-page

The title-page carries the title of the book and is often its most prominent typographic feature. The title of the book should be set in the same face as the text. The title itself should be in normal or bold type twice the size of the text type, and the author's name also in normal or bold one size larger than the text. A fine feeling for spacing is needed to compose the words pleasingly into groups in symmetrically arranged pages.

Always try to carry out your design with only two or three sizes of type, and to harmonize the typographic style with that of the rest of the book. Remember that the width, too, of the title-page text is determined by the type area of the body of the book. The visual weight of the page, especially with centred arrangements should always be in the top half of the page. This emphasis can be obtained by a grouping of the words or by using heavier type. Many minor elements, such as sub-titles, publisher's marks, dates, and edition numbers lend themselves readily to such grouping.

Still holding to this advice, it is possible to set the title square in the middle of the page. The entire lower half of the page must now be left free, and the author's name can well be set above the title with two or three blank lines in between. It is not advisable to let words drop below the middle of the page here. If you want to do this, make sure the balance is maintained by further emphasis of the upper section.

An asymmetrical title-page arrangement is more suitable than the classical form for technical and other specialist books. It can also be used for fiction, of course, but the designer's personal relationship to the contents of the work must influence the choice of method. Here again, the type area of the text body must be adhered to in the height and breadth. The further possibility of starting the titles on the centre-line of the page arises when the text is printed in two or more columns.

Imprint and copyright

The printer's imprint and copyright details are printed on the verso of the title-page. The copyright details may cover printing rights, translating rights, sale and resale regulations, and perhaps credits for cover design and so on. These details are usually set in small type (about 6 pt), and their design must be related to the remainder of the work. When the text itself is printed in type no larger than 8–9 pt, it may be possible to set these details in the same size.

Dedication

The dedication should likewise be related in type size and character to the main text and should be set on the top line of the type area. Dedications should always be short and simple and should be set in one line if possible.

Contents

The list of contents may be set in one or more columns. The chapter or section headings should be shown, together with their page numbers. Set the contents normally in the same type size as the text. If the list is very long and would thus take up too much space, use a smaller type. The layout of the contents page should follow that of the rest of the book.

Text page design
Type measure

Fictional works are nearly always set with the lines of text the full width of the type area. Technical, scientific, reference works, or dictionaries may be set in two or more columns for ease of orientation and reading. When the lines are long, it is confusing to the eye to search for the beginning of each new line in a full page of small type. This difficulty is overcome by splitting the area of type into columns, separated by a white space or perhaps even a column rule.

Chapter openings

Each new chapter should have a chapter heading to distinguish it. Set these in semi-bold type or in a larger size of the normal face.

When a chapter opens at the head of a new page, the text should be separated from the heading with a white space. This can be as little as one blank line or as much as half a side in the case of a new section or book in a larger work. The chapter openings must be the same throughout the book.

The first line of the chapter can be a quarter or a third of the way down the page or can be on the golden section of the height. The chapter heading can be on the first line of the type area. It is even possible to place the first line in the middle of the page with the heading at the top or one blank line above the text.

Chapter endings

The amount of text on the last page of a chapter will vary according to the length of the chapter. Avoid pages with less than three lines. If the book make-up shows such pages, either a sentence or two must be deleted from the chapter to remove the three odd lines, or conversely, one or two sentences must be added to the chapter to make the text a little longer. The printer can reduce the space taken up by a sentence to the extent of two or three words by a judicious reduction of the word spacing in a few lines. Write a note, "take back" in the margin. To get the opposite effect, write "take over" in the margin.

Marginal notes

Marginal notes, or hanging shoulder notes, are sometimes set alongside the text to facilitate quick reference to certain points. They are generally set centred in the margins or ranged inwards to the text. This last method is satisfactory on a right-hand page, but when used on a left-hand page it contradicts our western convention of writing left to right. To remove this objection, always range the marginal notes on both pages from the left. Set the notes one or two sizes smaller than the main text to avoid confusion with the latter and awkward divisions of words to fit the limited space.

The space between marginal notes and text is related to the line gauge of the text. For instance, if the text is set on a 10 pt body size, the distance between the text and notes should be likewise 10 pt. In cases where the marginal notes are used entirely instead of chapter headings they may also be set in bold type.

The marginal notes must be considered from the beginning as part of the type area of the text. The complete page, text notes, and margins, must be typographically well balanced.

Footnotes

Footnotes are explanatory or informative notes related to points in the text and are printed at the foot of the page or at the end of the chapter. The place in the text is marked by an asterisk or small reference number, which occurs again in the corresponding note. Footnotes are set one or two sizes smaller than the text. If set at the foot of the page, the notes must be considered as part of the type area and must be contained by the same measurements. The text is separated from the notes by one or two blank lines or by a thin ruled line. The notes should be leaded to achieve a similar grey tone to that of the text.

Index

The index provides a quick reference to individual subjects and their page numbers. The index is set in the same way as the list of contents, in a smaller type and perhaps in two or more columns. The subjects are listed alphabetically.

Cover and spine titles

The title on the cover may be a purely typographical design in keeping with the inside of the book, or it may be in contrast with it, having for instance, graphic devices, drawn lettering, or a facsimile of the author's signature. However, always bear in mind the type area of the text pages and dimension the cover design accordingly. On thin books, the spine title runs the length of the book. On thicker volumes, the lettering

A typographical treatment of a book front and spine

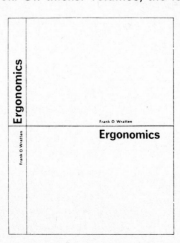

runs across the spine. The lettering should be consistent in style with the rest of the book and should
start at the height of the first line of the text type area,
or the optical centre of the spine.

On the cover are printed the title, the author's name,
and sometimes the publisher's mark. The spine carries
the title and author, and the volume number in the case
of books in a series.

Jacket

Originally the book jacket served simply to protect the
valuable binding from dust and dirt, and was plain and
unprinted. In the course of time it has developed into
a powerful advertising medium for the book and
author. It still retains the same form, being a loose

A book jacket related to the cover

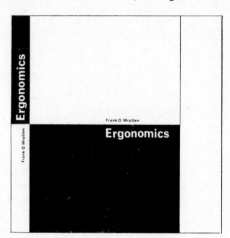

detachable folder, slipped over the book cover proper.
No rules can be given for the design of book jackets.
The designer has fairly complete freedom, the decision
to use a graphic or typographic solution, remaining
his. The method of printing, line block, half-tone block,
one or more colours, and so on, depends on the size
of the edition and the costs it can carry. Woodcuts,
linocuts, photographs, water colour, and pen drawings
can all be used to good effect, depending entirely on
the wish of the designer.

Casting off

It is possible to caculate simply the amount of printed
text any given manuscript will produce, and estimate
in advance how many pages a book will have. Get the

printer to set a few paragraphs of text with the right type and length of line. Now count the total number of letters and divide by the number of lines to find the average number of letters per line. Apply the same process to the manuscript. Next work out the number of letters on a printed page by counting the number of lines per page from the design and multiplying by the average number of letters per line. In the same way calculate the number of letters on a manuscript page. Multiply this by the number of manuscript pages to find the total number of letters in the manuscript. Finally, to find the number of pages of printed text divide this total by the number of letters on one side of printed text.

Example: the lines of printed text contain respectively 52, 56, 54, 55, 58 letters, a total of 275. There are 5 lines, so dividing by 5 gives an average of 55 letters per line. If there are 42 lines on each page this gives 2,310 letters per page. We deal with the manuscript in the same way. Assuming the average number of letters in 5 lines is 49 and that there are 38 lines on a page, gives us a total of 1,862 letters per page. In 180 manuscript pages there will be 335,160 letters. By dividing this total by the number of letters on a printed page we get the number of printed pages: $335,160 \div 2,310 = 145 \cdot 09$, thus we can say the manuscript will give 145 printed sides.

This calculation takes no account of title pages, chapter openings and endings, paragraph spacing, or blank pages, but it gives a rough check on whether the type size and the length of line are too large or too small, making the book too thick or too thin. You can alter the type size and calculate anew if you are not satisfied with the first results. To take account of illustrations work out the total area occupied by the pictures and add this to the number of printed pages.

Correction marks

Standard marks are used for the correction of printed matter which all compositors and printers can read. The general rule is to mark the error in the text and to repeat or explain the mark in the margin. This is necessary because when correcting printed matter, the compositor does not want to have to scan the whole text to pick out marks buried in the middle. Where the mark is made in the margin, attention is immediately drawn to the correction required.

MARGINAL MARK	MEANING	CORRESPONDING MARK IN TEXT
/	Correction is concluded	None
New matter followed by /	Insert in text the matter indicated in margin	⋏
℘	Delete	Strike through characters to be deleted
℘	Delete and close up	Strike through characters to be deleted and use mark
stet	Leave as printed	. . . . under characters to remain
ital.	Change to italic	―――― under characters to be altered
s.c.	Change to small capitals	══════ under characters to be altered
caps	Change to capital letters	≡≡≡under characters to be altered
c.& s.c.	Use capital letters for initial letters and small capitals for rest of words	≡≡≡under initial letters and ―――― under the rest of the words
bold	Change to bold type	∿∿∿under characters to be altered
l.c.	Change to lower case	Encircle characters to be altered
rom.	Change to roman type	Encircle character to be altered
w.f.	Wrong fount. Replace by letter of correct fount	Encircle character to be altered
9	Invert type	Encircle character to be altered
X	Change damaged character(s)	Encircle character(s) to be altered
�7 under character (e.g. ⤳).	Substitute or insert character(s) under which this mark is placed, in 'superior' position	/ through character or ⋏ where required
⋀ over character (e.g. ⤳ .)	Substitute or insert character(s) over which this mark is placed, in 'inferior' position	/ through character or ⋏ where required
underline	Underline word or words	―――― under words affected
⌣	Close up—delete space between characters	⌒linking characters

Extracted from the British Standards Institution table B.S. 1219:1958

MARGINAL MARK	MEANING	CORRESPONDING MARK IN TEXT
#	Insert space*	⅄
less #	Reduce space between lines*	(connecting lines to be closed up
eq #	Make space appear equal between words	| between words
less #	Reduce space between words*	| between words
letter #	Add space between letters*	ⅠⅠⅠⅠⅠ between tops of letters requiring space
trs	Transpose	between characters or words, numbered when necessary
centre	Place in centre of line	Indicate position with ⌐ ¬
□	Indent one em	
□□	Indent two ems	
⌐	Move matter to right	at left side of group to be moved
⌐	Move matter to left	at right side of group to be moved
take over	Take over character(s) or line to next line, column or page	
take back	Take back character(s) or line to previous line, column or page	
raise	Raise lines*	over lines to be moved / under lines to be moved
lower	Lower lines*	over lines to be moved / under lines to be moved
‖	Correct the vertical alignment	‖
≡	Straighten lines	through lines to be straightened
n.p.	Begin a new paragraph	⌐ before first word of new paragraph
run on	No fresh paragraph here	between paragraphs
⊙	Substitute or insert full stop	/ through character or ⅄ where required

*Amount of space and/or length of line may be included.

129

ILLUSTRATIONS

Catalogues, leaflets, programmes, and sometimes even literary works, would be inconceivable without illustrations. The photograph is the most forceful medium for advertising. A good photograph is the best way to show an object or an idea realistically and objectively. A "good" photograph is not necessarily the one showing the best subject in the best artistic taste, but the one whose message is seen and recognized most easily. The photograph must also be technically perfect: a brilliant print is essential for clean reproduction. Good line drawings are bound to reproduce clearly provided they are not reduced so much in scale that the finer lines become too thin.

Full-page illustrations

The simplest picture layout is the full-page layout. The most sensible place for a photograph is on the right-hand page of a spread: the right-hand pages are seen first when you look through a book. There are two ways of printing an illustration on a page. It may be "bled off", going right to the edges of the paper, or it may come within the type area with a margin all round. In a bled-off illustration, as with all printed matter, allowance must be made for trimming. This amounts to about $\frac{1}{8}$–$\frac{3}{16}$ in. (3–5 mm.) and of course cuts into the picture. This loss can be counteracted in a photograph or drawing by extending the illustration a little. The case is different for reproductions of paintings or documents. In this case it is better to contain the illustration within the type area. This method has the advantage of not presenting difficulties with the trimming, or the location of the folio and any captions.

Example: In a leaflet to A5 size the possibilities are as follows: Portrait illustrations can take the width of the type measure. The height can be up to the depth of page minus the number of lines needed for the caption and a two-line space in between. Landscape illustrations can also take the full width of the type measure. As before, the caption will remain at the

Type area plan and scheme for placing the
pictures

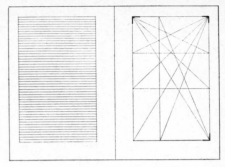

bottom of the area; the white space in between does
no harm.

Captions should be set in the same type size or one
size smaller than the text and should always be set at
the bottom of the type area with the last line at the
same level as the last lines of main text.

Layout of illustrations

You will not always have the good fortune to receive
illustrations all of the same proportions. For instance,
photographers will often produce pictures which for
various reasons must have proportions totally un-
related to the normal photographic paper sizes. This
is even more so with woodcuts, linocuts, etchings,
paintings, and so on, whose proportions are

Scheme for placing illustrations in a
square type area

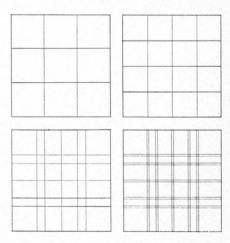

131

determined by aesthetic considerations. In such cases it is unthinkable to alter the proportions of the work to suit your needs.

You must therefore work out a design enabling you to integrate illustrations with widely different proportions. For example: you may fit illustrations into each right-hand page of a book so that they are bounded by the size of the type area. Here you could use the upper right-hand corner of the type area as a reference point and set each picture into this corner initially. Now you can enlarge landscape pictures until they fill the space horizontally. Portrait pictures can be enlarged downwards until they have reached the limit set by the depth of page minus the space for the caption. The second dimension of all the illustrations will of course depend

Some arrangements of illustrations in a square type area

Arrangement plan for illustrations in a type area with proportions 3 : 4

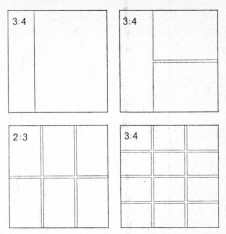

on the proportions of the original and the degree of enlarging or reducing.

Photographs can have many proportions, depending on how much of the negative is reproduced or how much of the paper is used. Standard photographic paper sizes are in the proportion of roughly 3 : 4. Do not use photographs larger than whole plate ($6\frac{1}{2} \times 8\frac{1}{2}$ in.) as you will have great trouble sending them unscathed through the post. Try, too, not to use anything smaller than quarter plate. It is difficult to make a good block from such a small original.

Illustrations among the text

Sometimes drawings or photographs must appear among the text. In this case, adjust the size of the

Arrangement plan for illustrations in a type area with proportions 2 : 3

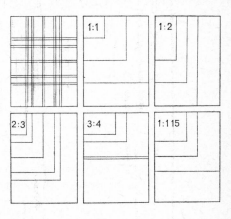

Illustrations

Arrangement plan for illustrations in a type area with proportions 2 : 3

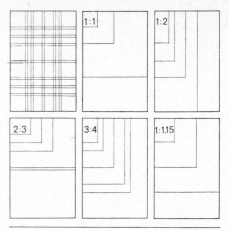

picture until it is as wide as the type measure. The height will now vary according to the proportion of the original. The picture must now be trimmed perhaps a fraction of an inch to ensure that two or three lines space remain between it and the text. The height of the illustration must also be a multiple of the line gauge. If it is at all possible, standardize the size of such illustrations appearing in the middle of the text. But to be safe, work out a type area layout capable of taking two or three sizes of illustration. Try to fix the position of illustration on the page and keep to this arrangement throughout the book.

It is typographically wrong to completely "run round" an illustration with text. In addition such text is difficult both to set and to read. Also to be avoided are oval, circular, or rounded illustrations. These are contrary to the basic system of composing and cannot be considered satisfactory. They bring tolerancing difficulties and there is a risk of rising spaces as a result of ill-fitting type.

Drawings

Technical and free drawings should be designed so that they may be easily contained in a rectangle or a square without leaving too much empty space. Awkwardly shaped spaces in a drawing can seldom be filled with text and destroy the unity of the page. Check your own drawings before sending them to the blockmaker by pencilling in the intended outlines lightly. You need give the blockmaker the dimension of one side only.

Background tone

For certain applications you may want to use a photograph of an object with no background, or perhaps only cast a shadow to establish perspective. This shadow may be genuine or it may be air-brushed in later.

A uniform white background (or no background) or a neutral tone may likewise be achieved in the photograph itself or it may be painted, or air-brushed in later. The background must be sprayed in if it is to appear as a light grey tone. This is printed by the finest points on the half-tone block.

If the subject is to be completely cut out with the background pure white, the parts of the block not wanted are etched or routed away. Before sending your original to the blockmaker you must indicate what portions are to be removed. Cover the drawing with tracing paper and draw round these areas. Shade in the areas and write "cut out" on the sheet.

Be sparing and careful in your use of this method. Apply it only to suitable photographs. It is not in keeping with the character of a photograph to cut out parts. The method can be used well with illustrations of technical subjects, machine parts, products, and the like, but the result is not pleasing when applied to natural subjects such as people. The soft outlines become hard and mechanical, giving a petrified appearance to the subject. Cut-out photographs are integrated with the text in the same way as drawings.

Choosing picture size

The originals of black-and-white or coloured drawings or photographs are sent to the blockmaker who will make printing plates or blocks from them. These blocks will have different heights and widths according to the method of printing used.

The drawings or photographs may be prepared for "same size" reproduction. It is however very easy to reduce large drawings when making blocks, and to a certain extent small drawings can be enlarged.

If you want to retain the same proportions of a picture but to reduce it in size to fit on the page, draw a diagonal through two opposite corners with pencil on the back of the picture. Now measure out the new height or width from one of these corners and construct a horizontal or vertical to cut the diagonal. The length of this line will be the new reduced length of the

Illustrations

Proportional enlargement and reduction
of a format with sides of a proportion
3 : 4
1 Original format
2 Linear reduction 2 : 1
3 Linear enlargement 1 : 1.5

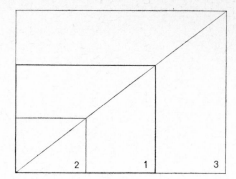

other side of the picture. You can also enlarge pictures
proportionally in the same way. Stick the original down
on a sheet of paper, if possible in the bottom left
corner. Extend the diagonal of the picture on the paper.
Draw in the determining dimension as before and
extend a vertical to cross the diagonal line, giving the
length of the second side. In both cases mark in the
new dimensions of the picture on the original.

A straight or circular slide rule can be used to calculate the new sizes of reduced or enlarged pictures.
There are three known dimensions and one unknown
in such a sum.

Example: a picture measuring 20×16 in. must be
reduced so that the long side measures 10 in. If the
unknown side is *x* cm. long the relation can be set out
as follows:

20 : 16=10 : *x*

then $x = \dfrac{16 \times 10}{20} = 8$ in.

The small side of the reduced picture must then be
8 in. long. More complicated cases can be easily
reckoned with a circular slide-rule. This consists of
two concentric discs with a scale of numbers moving
against one another. To find the new width of a reduced
picture, line up the dimension of the long side on the
outer scale against the dimension of the short side on
the inner scale. Now you can read off the new width on
the inside scale against the new length on the outer
scale. There are no units on the scales, and you must
always work out the position of the decimal point

A circular calculator set at 2 : 1

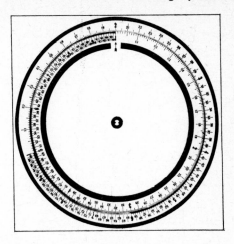

yourself. You can of course reckon in English, metric, or typographical units, but you must stick to one type throughout a calculation. You enlarge pictures in the same way. Always check the calculated result against your layout sketch. If the two proportions do not tally you can calculate the necessary proportions of the original and trim the picture accordingly, provided the picture allows it.

Masking a picture

You can determine the best area of the picture to use by masking out with strips of paper or by moving a pre-cut mask over the picture. Do not cut off the unused areas of the picture on any account. You will usually re-file the original photographs after blockmaking. As these are usually made on a standard size of paper, cutting to other sizes would mean additional work making new prints.

A practical method is to cut two L-shaped masks out of stiff card. Lay the picture on a soft paper underlay and then mask out the required picture using the two corner masks. Now press a fairly sharp pencil into the corners of the masks to mark the size of the picture. These marks will show through on the back of the print because of the soft underlay. Check that the edges of the new picture are at right-angles and draw in the sides with pencil. Press back the four corner points with your thumbnail. Hold the print up to a strong light and look through from the back to check the new borders and then mark in the new dimensions.

Illustrations

Corner masks of white card for
determining the picture size

With full-page illustrations with bled edges, remember that about $\frac{1}{8}$ in. (3 mm.) will be trimmed off after printing. This means the original must be $\frac{1}{8}$ in. larger on each side that bleeds. This extra paper will be trimmed off later, ensuring that the picture fills the complete page. The dimensions may be indicated on the back of the photograph, but a surer way of indicating the borders is to lay a mask over the original. This method is clearer to the blockmaker and makes his work easier. Mount the original on a large sheet of paper using rubber solution or adhesive tape; cut a mask of thin paper showing a correctly proportioned section of the picture and hiding the unwanted portions. Lay the mask over the print and stick it down in place. It is only necessary to fix the upper edge leaving the

Trimming a printed and folded sheet.
About $\frac{1}{8}$ in. is trimmed off three sides to
open the fold.

sheet loose at the bottom edge. A sheet of tracing paper can be attached over the print in the same way. Here you can draw in the required proportions and also indicate areas to be retouched or corrected with suitable remarks in pencil on the transparent sheet.

Instructions to blockmaker

It is practical to make all the enlargements or reductions according to a layout fitting in with the type area plan. A layout is a sketch showing the type columns, chapter headings and all the illustrations.

Number each illustration in the layout and write the corresponding number on the back of each print or drawing for the blockmaker. You may perhaps even sketch in the outlines of each illustration in the layout: a well-ordered layout makes the subsequent sorting of text and illustration much easier.

The block sizes are either the full width of the type area or a certain proportion of it. Various constant dimensions result from the use of a type area plan and the resulting illustration layout which determines at least one side of the block which fills this space (see page 130).

Give full instructions to the blockmaker, preferably on the back of the original, as follows:

1. Insert the required dimensions of the block on the back of the original. State the units as well as numbers.
2. Note the desired screen ruling (e.g. 133 screen, 120 screen, etc.).
3. If the block is to be cut out or vignetted, make a note on the original to this effect.
4. For fine-screened blocks, say whether a zinc or a copper plate is wanted.
5. State how you wish the blocks to be delivered: mounted on wood or metal, with or without bevels, and so on. These questions should be discussed in advance with the printer.
6. If you wish to duplicate the blocks, arrange with the printer how this is to be done: stereos or electros, nickel or chrome plated, 11 pt thick or type-high, and of course, how many duplicates are needed.
7. It is advisable to give the blockmaker some sheets of the paper to be used for printing on which he can take proofs. This will help to avoid mistakes or disappointments later.
8. It is preferable to supply all the photographs on a uniform size of paper (e.g. $6\frac{1}{2} \times 8\frac{1}{2}$ in. or 8×10 in.).

If it is necessary to retouch a background into the picture it is advisable to have plenty of white border, otherwise the retoucher will have to lay a transparent film over the print and spray over that. This makes the work more difficult and dearer.

The golden section

The golden section, or golden mean is the division of a line so that the proportion of the smaller to the larger part is that of the larger part to the whole. One way of constructing the golden section on a line AB is as follows:

Draw a perpendicular BC with a length half that of AB. Join A and C to form a triangle. With centre C,

Constructing the golden section
EB : AE=1 : 1.618

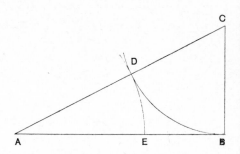

draw an arc through B to cut AC at point D. Finally, with centre A, draw an arc through D to cut AB at E. Point E divides the line so that BE : AE=AE : AB. The ratio of the shorter to the longer part is 1 : 1·618.

GRAPHIC DESIGN

Trademarks

The most difficult yet most interesting problem of graphic design is the development of a trade mark. Taking a look at ancient Chinese seals, we see that the seal cutter has changed the thick and thin brush strokes of the original signs to thin lines of even thickness. The reason is that the varying thickness could not be cut as easily in the jade or metal used for the block. The cutter has simplified the written signs formally, in some cases making geometric devices of them. Today, trademarks and signs play an important part in communication and are not designed solely for printing on paper. We must bear in mind that the mark may be moulded or cast into plastic or metal products, stencilled on packages, burned into wooden cases, or even erected as a neon sign.

The sign must be simple and forceful. These conditions can often be successfully fulfilled when the sign takes the form of one of the basic geometrical figures—circle, equilateral triangle, or square. The sign must have the character of a symbol: the message should be clear to the onlooker without explanatory text. If, however, text is used to emphasize the meaning

Chinese official seals

of the symbol, it should be of a purely typographical character and suitable for placing below, above, or at the side of the symbol. The advantage of this variant is seen when the symbol is set alternatively with the firm and product names. Here you can freely alter the proportions of symbol and text or change the spacing of the two.

Design the symbol so that it can be enlarged or reduced without difficulty. Remember that fine lines may break up, and small negative areas may be filled in if the reduction is considerable.

Another big advantage of choosing a geometrically constructed symbol is that manual reproduction is possible. The symbol can be drawn to any size on delivery vans, posters, and perhaps buildings easily

Examples of trademarks based on:
1 The square
2 An equilateral triangle
3 A circle
4 Combined forms
5 Line forms
6 Monograms

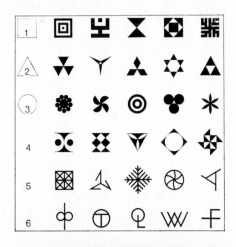

This arrow serves as a traffic sign. The formal division of the rectangular field by the integrated arrow is very effective

142

Gothic stonemason's signs in St. Stephen's
Cathedral, Vienna. The construction
lines determine the form of the sign
as a circle with inscribed square

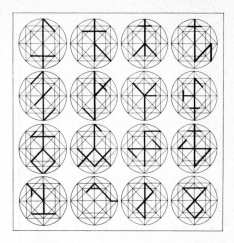

and quickly with simple tools, without recourse to photographic processes. You must of course fix the *proportions* of the symbol, but the actual dimensions can be different for each application.

The character of the symbol will vary from business to business: a printer's house-mark will have a different character to the trade-mark of a building contractor. The symbol will not have merely a momentary effect, but should hold its own for perhaps more than a decade without losing its power. Such conditions can only be fulfilled by a fundamental process of design development calculated to reduce the symbol to its essentials and produce a convincing result.

Monograms

A simpler form of symbol is the monogram. This is a symbol formed by two or more letters, usually the initials of an individual or a business. The complete name of a product or firm can also be turned into a symbol by the use of distinctive lettering. The complete image is important here, but avoid using standard types or making your symbol similar to others. Do not distort letters or words to form pictures of the product named. All such attempts are forced and in bad taste.

Record sleeves

Record sleeves provide an exciting and exacting exercise for a graphic designer. The possibilities are almost unlimited, the only two limitations being in the size and perhaps the method of opening.

JATP presents

The Modern Jazz Quartet

John Lewis
Milt Jackson
Percy Heath
Connie Kay

The front and reverse sides of a record
sleeve

The Modern Jazz Quartet

The record itself is protected by a thin paper or plastic envelope which in turn is contained in the stiff card sleeve. A coated card is used and is folded and glued (sometimes stitched) into sleeve form after printing. The finished sleeve may be toughened by laminating a layer of Cellophane on to the surface. Sometimes a thin printed sheet of paper is mounted on a plain card sleeve.

Record sleeves usually carry a black-and-white or coloured illustration on the front, together with the title of the works, the composers, players, the and the record company's name or mark. The back is usually occupied by a description of the players or composer and the works on the record. Often, especially on jazz records, the names of the players are given priority over the title of the music. The basic rules of graphic design apply as much to record sleeves as to posters, advertisements, and other items. A purely typographic solution to the design of a record sleeve can also be successful.

Packaging

A package not only protects a product from wear and tear, but also helps to sell the product to the customer. In contrast to all the design exercises mentioned so far, packages are three-dimensioned. There are many problems to be faced here. The package must display the name of the product and the producer on all sides, it must be as compact as possible, it must be stackable, and it must be transportable. The stacking requirement often favours a unit or modular design of the package, so that the packages can be built up like bricks.

There are many new customer requirements to be dealt with—the package must be airtight or watertight, tear-resistant or heat-proof, and all of these play a part in the final solution. While designing you must show that your chosen material can withstand all the wear and tear to which it will later be subjected. Alkaline solutions attack the printing ink and can even eat away a poor-quality paper. Strong sunshine can likewise destroy the colours. The package must always withstand tests twice as severe as anything it will receive in use without showing signs of wear.

Chromo paper or card is good for cartons, and may be strengthened after printing with varnish or Cellophane laminate. You will do well to make a collection of different types of material suitable for packages.

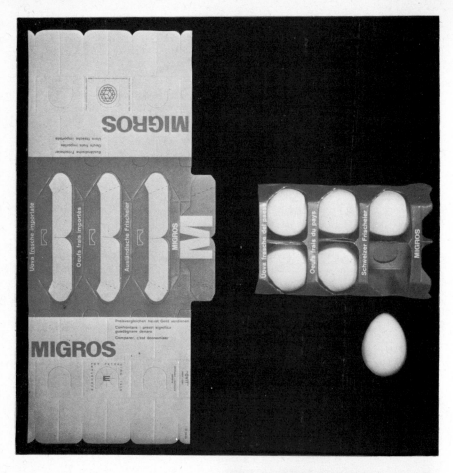

Folded package for eggs. The eggs are
visible but cannot fall out

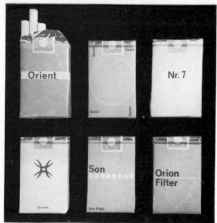

Designs for cigarette packets

146

Stages in the folding and assembly of a
cushion-shaped package

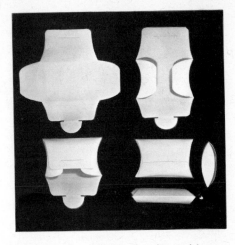

This will be of great help in solving fresh problems,
especially when an original design is called for.

The outside of the package must carry clear information about its contents: the customer must see at a
glance what is inside. Good solutions can be achieved
both photographically and purely typographically. The
field of package design is so large and varied that you
must understand the materials fully and let your initial
ideas ripen slowly into the final design. You must ask
the question "What must I sell?". Can you turn the
natural form of the product into a symbol? In what
colours or colour range must you carry out the design?
A cigarette package and a carton for a bottle of per-
fume must have entirely different characters. They
may be exactly the same size and shape, and must
therefore be distinguishable by the graphics alone.

Use to the full the possibilities of typography. The
character of a product can be unmistakably described
by skilful use of the right type. There are many simple
ornamental motives which can be combined in a
variety of colours and forms with lettering to produce a
host of designs.

Naturalistic illustrations of the goods are favoured
in the food industry. Packages with Cellophane win-
dows are used to display some foodstuffs, and with
the growth of frozen foods come a new range of
hermetically-sealed transparent packings which can be
printed excellently with special inks. With briefly
printed cooking instructions and so on, this type of
package gives the maximum amount of information
about the contents.

Tinned products must be treated differently. The tins are either decorated with a stuck-on label or are printed directly with ink. If you want to use a naturalistic illustration, this must be a photograph. Hand drawings just do not come up to the same standard, and do not give a correct impression of the product.

It is wrong to assume that a package is effective only when it is cluttered up with all sorts of decoration, pictures, and type. A well-ordered simple design is likely to have far more selling power than its over-cluttered neighbour.

Endpapers and wrapping papers

Endpapers are the leaves at the beginning and end of a book. The first and last leaves are pasted to the inside of the covers. Nowadays endpapers are very rarely decorated, but sometimes examples may be seen in children's or travel books. Here the designs usually take the form of themes from the story or travel maps.

More often you will see paper-backed books with a decorated cover. This is usually printed with a repeating design, the publisher's mark, or some motif based on an episode from the text. The book title is often stuck on a separate label as on school exercise books.

Wrapping papers and cartons are used by many trades for different products, and many choose to use a decorative paper. This decoration is printed as a repeating design on paper or card. House symbols, product names and brand marks, slogans, or even an illustration of the contents are suitable motifs for the design.

An end-paper printed from two linocuts

Wrapping paper is printed on the roll and cut to size as required. Cartons are often delivered flat, but pre-stamped, and are folded up and slotted or stapled together before use. The manufacturer's name and details of the contents are often applied on a separate label later. The design motif may be hand drawn or be a lino- or woodcut print. The repeat is constructed as described on page 158.

Labels

Gummed labels are stuck on bottles to give details of the contents and manufacturer. Champagne, vermouth, and brandy are some of the bottles which carry extra labels as a means of enriching the appearance and apparent value of the bottle. These are stuck around the neck of the bottle.

Your design of a label will be affected by the economics and capabilities of the production process available. Bottling plants are generally keyed to definite processes. The labels are printed in sheets and stamped out later.

When deciding on the size for a label, bear in mind the sizes which can be cut on the stamping machine. Simple shapes are of course preferable to complicated ones, as the machine process is easier. Considerable freedom remains for the graphic design of the label. Do not make the label too large, and above all do not let it grow too wide, otherwise the lettering will extend too far round the bottle. This will make it impossible to read without turning the bottle. Ideally the whole label should be legible at a glance.

Beer bottles with enamelled lettering

Enamel may be used to print a label directly on the bottle itself. This method is especially useful for returnable bottles, as it is very durable. It is resistant to acids and alkalies, and to weathering and wear, and need not be renewed every time the bottle is returned and refilled. The design is silk-screened on to the glass and is baked on at a temperature of about 1,100°F (600°C).

Practical design

Designing for printing implies and demands the cleanest and tidiest work. Accurate dimensioning and exact black-and-white or coloured drawing are indispensable for good results. The worst fault, often brought about through carelessness, is that no right-angle in the design is absolutely true. This can be corrected later, but only by sometimes drastic trimming of the design. This, of course, can alter the work considerably. There are so many things which can go wrong with a design when it is not done properly that it will be better to look in more detail at some of the main points to be watched when executing a design.

Preparing the materials

First you must have a good working surface. For normal work a drawing board or an accurate piece of plywood will do. A large drawing board laid across two trestles will do excellent service when you are doing large jobs. You can use the board horizontally as a table, and mount it on an easel to view the work from a distance every now and then. Stiff drawing paper or card is suitable for normal jobs, and thicker card will do for posters too.

There are special poster papers in various colours suitable for poster work. These papers do not cockle much when wet. However, they have a very porous surface, and it is difficult to lay on paint evenly, especially when using watercolours. This difficulty can be overcome by priming the surface with a coat of cellulose or emulsion size (see page 201). In special cases you can use other materials such as wood, hardboard, cardboard, or linen as a painting surface. They, too, must be suitably prepared.

Stretching drawing paper

The finished art work should be absolutely flat and even. For this reason, when working with water-soluble paints, it is as well to stretch the paper evenly before starting work. Wet stretching is the best method. It does not matter if you use trimmed paper or cut it yourself from the roll. Cut the paper generously to size and take the machine direction of the paper into account (see page 182). When damp, the paper will stretch most at right-angles to the machine direction and will shrink most in the same direction on drying, so do not cut too sparingly on these sides.

There are two ways of stretching paper:

1. If your paper is to cover the whole drawing-board, cut it to about 1 in. (2–3 cm.) bigger on each side. Lay the paper on the board with the smooth or coated side downwards and fold up the edges to form a sort of tray. Damp the back of the sheet well with a sponge until it is thoroughly soaked. Spread the folded up edges with dextrin, cellulose, or resin glue. Now turn the paper over, and press down the sticky borders to the edges of the drawing-board. Just in case the glue does not hold, push in a few drawing pins along each side. The paper will dry and stretch taut like a drum skin. The surface is ideal for working on. It may buckle a little under the paint, but will flatten again as it dries.

2. If your paper is smaller than the drawing-board, stick it down with sticky tape. Cut the paper about 1 in. (2–3 cm.) larger than you need and damp it well on the back. Turn it over and stick the edges well down with gummed strip. Again, with larger sheets, it is as well to reinforce the gummed strip with drawing pins, and a double layer of strip can do no harm. A large sheet of paper may stretch so tight that the gummed strip tears away.

As already mentioned, there is no need to stretch poster papers. However, it is better to pin the edges down about every 4 in. (10 cm.) as the paper will always buckle slightly with moisture.

Marking up with a T-square

If you have stretched the paper well, the surface will be flat and without folds. You need have no fears that the paper will stretch or shrink during the work. Now you must mark in your drawing area with a T-square. Always press the T-square firmly against the edge of the board. Line the square up on to the mark, run your left hand along the straightedge, and then press the T-square hard up to the board again. This is the only sure way of ensuring that the T-square is laid true

Using the drawing board:
1 A T-square with fixed head
2 T-square with adjustable head
3 45° set square
4 30/60° set square

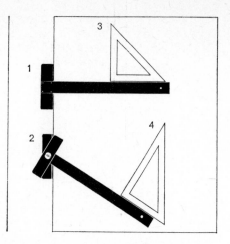

against the board edge. When this is not so, the lines will never be exactly parallel, and it takes a long time to check back later when you discover the mistake.

Do not line the T-square up from the bottom edge of the board to draw the vertical lines, but use a set-square. This is more exact, as you can never be sure that the two edges of the board are absolutely true, and the board may have been warped by moisture from the paper stretching.

Using tracing paper

It is a good idea to cover the stretched paper with a sheet of tracing paper. Cut this to size and fix it down with pins or sticky tape. Trace through the borders of the drawing. You can now sketch in the details of your design on this cover sheet. This is a great help when your design is not quite clear and you must do a bit of alteration. You can draw in and rub out as often as you need without spoiling the final sheet. The tracing paper is useful too when you want to enlarge or reduce a sketch before transferring it on to the final sheet.

Enlarging and reducing

There are several ways of enlarging or reducing a drawing:
1. *Gridding.* This is a method of transferring a sketch without using any special instruments. Draw a light grid of squares over the original sketch. Over the tracing paper overlay on the drawing board draw a similar grid, proportionately larger or smaller. Now,

Squaring a sheet. The original grid is
enlarged proportionally on to the
sheet for the final design

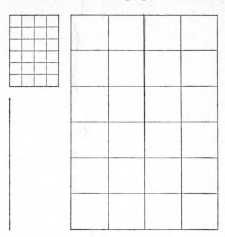

A pantograph

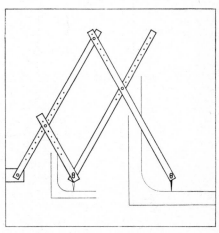

using the lines as an easy reference, you can transfer
the sketch on to the board square by square.

2. *Using a pantograph.* This method is easier and more
exact. You can enlarge or reduce a drawing up to 10 : 1.
The pantograph is a movable parallelogram made of
wooden or metal arms. These arms can be linked together at various points to give different degrees of
enlargement or reduction.

Screw the pantograph down to the lower left corner
of the drawing board. Now trace around the outlines
of the original with the tracing point on one link of the
parallelogram. The drawing point on the end of the
pantograph will then trace out an enlarged drawing.

3. *Projecting with an epidiascope.* An epidiascope is an
apparatus for direct projection of pictures. With it you

can project drawings horizontally or vertically straight on to the drawing board, and then draw round the outlines or paint in the design directly. This is by far the simplest method of enlarging or reducing and takes infinitely less time than the gridding method.

Tracing through

After the design is finished on the tracing paper it must be transferred on to the drawing sheet. You can rub over the back of the tracing paper with a soft pencil or powder a stick of carbon on to the paper and rub it over with cotton wool. Then replace the sheet and go over the drawing with a hard pencil, pressing the carbon underneath through on to the white paper.

It is quicker and less messy to use carbon paper. Lay a sheet of carbon paper under the tracing paper and go over the drawing with a hard pencil or ballpoint pen.

Montage with coloured paper

Coloured paper montage is suitable for designs with large flat areas of colour. Try to arrange with a printer for a supply of coloured paper. Ask the printer, if, after each run of offset printing, he will use the remaining ink to print a few sheets of paper. If all goes well you can build up a collection of sheets of all colours, which are useful for all sorts of jobs.

These papers are particularly good for making designs for offset printing. The correct reproduction of unmixed colours is ensured, and even mixed tones can be quite accurately reproduced.

If you cannot get a supply of paper from the printer, you can buy normal coloured papers or make your own by spraying or brushing tempera colour. Use rubber solution to mount the sheets on the design. Draw the outlines of the areas to be coloured inverted on the back of the coloured sheet. Cut this shape out with about $\frac{1}{8}$ in. (3 mm.) to spare all round, using scissors or a sharp modelling knife. Spread rubber solution on both surfaces to be stuck. After about 2–3 minutes the solution will be dry and you will see more shiny patches. Lay the coloured paper in place and press it down lightly. Rubber solution is a contact adhesive and the surfaces will stick immediately. The edges of the paper will overlap the area on the design, and are trimmed together, to ensure an exact fit.

When sticking large areas, it is easy to get bubbles or folds in the paper; these cannot be removed and do not improve the work. There is a neat way of avoiding this. Lay a sheet of tracing paper over the design when the adhesive is dry. Pull this back to expose a small strip of glue at one side. Lay the coloured paper in position (you can see the drawing through the tracing paper) and press it down on the exposed adhesive. Now slowly pull the tracing paper away, pressing down the coloured paper after it. This method will give you smooth areas of colour.

Finally, trim the overlapping edges of the paper with a sharp knife. Do not cut through the base paper. The surplus strips can be pulled away. Rub down the edges of the coloured paper well. If you cut exactly, the edges of the different papers will fit together like inlay work. A straightedge is good for cutting straight lines, a cutting compass for circles, and a french curve for curves.

If you stick down the paper wrongly, it is possible to remove it. Use a little benzine to dissolve stubborn rubber.

The chief drawback with rubber solution is that it does not stick the papers together so firmly as a paste or glue. Thus you cannot roll the work at all: the paper separates and you get bubbles and folds. The great advantage is that rubber solution does not distort the paper in any way. You need not stretch the paper first before carrying out the design. Surplus rubber can be removed later simply by rubbing over the work with your finger or a cloth. Rubber solution makes a much cleaner job than is possible with paste.

Tissue paper work

Another method of introducing colour into a design is to lay on areas of coloured tissue paper. Tissue paper is obtainable in a wide range of fresh, clear, and almost transparent colours. Do not use the largest sheets, as it is very difficult to stick them down evenly. Cut or tear the shapes you need from the tissue, and paste them well with dextrine or cellulose paste, using an old newspaper as an underlay. Stick down the pasted paper immediately, and press it down lightly with a cloth. Take care to get the paper in the right position first time, as the colour will run out of the paper very easily and leave marks if you try to move the tissue. Finally press the surplus moisture out of the tissue with a sheet of blotting paper. When you lay one tissue over another, the colour of the first will show through.

Coloured foils

The methods described up to now are suitable only for designs with covering or semi-transparent colours. For designs to be printed with transparent inks giving subtractive colour mixing, you must use transparent foils. Use rubber solution for sticking. Thin foils can be cut with scissors or a sharp knife; score thicker sheets with a needle, and then you can break them cleanly along the scored lines. Spread rubber solution over the foil and stick it down wet. Slide the piece around until it is in the right place and then, holding one edge down firmly, press out the surplus glue with a ruler edge. You can remove solution from round the edges of the area as soon as it is dry with your finger or a cloth.

With thin foils you may find that small air bubbles have formed under the surface. You can flatten these by pricking them with a pin and then pressing them down well. You can stick down thin plastic or metal foils on your designs in exactly the same way.

Self-adhesive foils and tints

You can obtain several kinds of self-adhesive foils with transparent or covering colours or large range of textures suitable for smaller jobs. These foils have a protective backing sheet. To fill in an area, pull off the backing sheet and lay the foil on the drawing. Press it down lightly with your fingers, and cut round the required outline. Rub the necessary part down firmly now and then pull away the surplus foil. Replace this on the backing sheet to prevent the adhesive becoming dirty.

Using tempera colours

Several points must be watched when using tempera or casein colours. The colours must be thoroughly mixed so that there are no bits of unmixed colour which could cause smears on the work. Mix plenty of colour for large areas; it is better to have too much than too little. When a colour runs out in the middle of a job it is difficult to remix exactly the same tone. A little poster white mixed in with the colour helps a lot. The colour will spread much more evenly than one without white.

You can use the following methods for laying on a flat area:

1. This method is suitable for large designs, such as posters, where you can get to work with a good wide brush. Mask out the borders with sticky tape, having first run the tape over your finger to remove excess stickiness. Press down the tape well. Now you can lay on the paint without worrying about going over the edges. When the colour is dry, pull off the masking tape.

2. For smaller jobs, where you can use a small brush and freely flowing paint, draw round the outlines first with a ruling pen loaded with colour, and then fill out the area with a brush. You may have to thin the colour with a little water to make it flow in the ruling pen.

Drawings for the blockmaker

Designs for printing with flat areas of colour may be made into half-tone blocks or, more usually, into line blocks. In the four-colour half-tone process the colours are separated by photographing through filters and a screen (see page 31). When used for line blocks, this method does not always give satisfactory results. The flat, even areas of colour are difficult to separate. The blockmaker will normally insert an extra drawing stage into the process.

This is not always done to the full satisfaction of the graphic designer, and you will avoid any unpleasant surprises if you provide the blockmaker with your own component drawings. The method is as follows: mark registration poin.s on the drawing, say in the middle of both the short sides. Lay a sheet of transparent foil over the drawing and trace the registration marks through.

Foil with a matt surface is better than a glossy one. Now trace through and paint in with black tempera or brown opaque colour all the parts of the design which have one of the basic colours. The use of brown opaque paint, the same as that used for masking negatives, is good when the design is the same size as the final block.

The drawings can be transferred straight on to the block without intermediate reproduction. This method is often used with designs suitable for silk-screen reproduction (see page 80). Each basic colour is transferred in black (or brown) on to a separate transparent screen in the same way as on the design.

Straight lines are drawn with a straightedge, circles with a compass, and curves with a french curve. Freer drawings, such as brushwork, are traced through in the same way as the original so long as they are to be reproduced from line blocks.

The separate colour drawings are then reproduced separately, numbered for printing, and made up into blocks. The printer starts with the lightest colour, yellow for instance, goes on to the next darkest, such as red, and so on, finishing with black. Subtractive colour mixing occurs where two colours overlap: for instance, transparent blue printed over yellow gives green.

Sometimes the prints from two blocks do not co-incide exactly on the paper. This can happen when the paper stretches or moves slightly between impressions. It is disturbing when a white border shows through at the junction of two colours. This can be avoided by taking the possibility into account in the colour drawings. Let us take an example. You have a design in which a yellow disc stands on a red ground. You can now make the yellow disc slightly larger than the hole in the red ground, or make the negative hole in the red smaller. In both cases the red ground will be printed after the yellow disc and will overlap slightly all round. This will take care of any slight inaccuracies in the printing. In no case should the colours overlap more than about $\frac{1}{64}$ in. (0·3 mm.): a dark band of colour would be just as disturbing as a white strip.

Stencilling

This is a method suitable for smaller designs such as repeating designs or textured surfaces. A stencil mask is cut from stiff card for each colour. Use a sharp knife for cutting. For longer runs it may be necessary to protect the stencils with a coat of varnish. Special stencil brushes, with short, stiff bristles are used. Tempera colour is used just as it comes from the tube. Mix the colours with a palette knife on a glass sheet, and then spread the paint out on to the sheet. Load the brush by dabbing it vertically into the spread colour. Position the stencil on the design and apply the colour to the area with the same dabbing movement. Work inwards from the borders or the colour will creep under the edges of the stencil. If the colour dries on the glass plate, while you are working, thin it again with a little water. Oil paints are very good for stencil work. Use the colours straight from the tube. You may add a little drying oil to the colours to accelerate the drying.

Repeat designs

Symbols, vignettes, and other small motifs can be printed in several ways and combined with one another to form borders or areas of texture. Such devices are often made as woodcuts or linocuts, or are reproduced photographically or with stencils.

The design must "repeat": in other words, it must fit together so that the dividing lines between units are not visible. Check that the design repeats as follows: Take an impression, photocopy, or tracing of the design and draw in its rectangular or square outline. Mark the corners with registration points. Cut the design accurately into four quarters. Exchange the four quarters diagonally so that the four corner registration marks are now together in the middle. Stick the parts down in this position. When the design is repeated, the outside edges must tally, as they were originally together.

You can now make any alterations necessary to make sure that the new joints in the middle fit well. Whether you return the quarters to their original positions, or leave them as they are, the design will repeat evenly when printed continuously in a grid. Each field of the grid must of course have the same dimensions as the repeat. The registration points mark the corners of the grid. The size of the repeat for printing paper continuously in the roll is dependent on the width and circumference of the printing rollers. You must obtain these measurements first from the printer.

Using tempera and casein colours

Tempera and casein colours are suitable for many types of design work. You can overpaint tempera colours several times, but not indefinitely. It is better to mix a little binder or casein adhesive with the paint if you intend to overpaint a lot (see page 155). Sometimes an overpainted colour will show through time and time again. This is a sure sign that a dye has been added to the colour. Here you must either remove the offending colour with a sponge or mix binder with the covering colour. You can now lay on the paint without danger of the undercoat dissolving and showing through. Again, you must not lay the colour on too thickly, or it may start to flake off when dry.

You can use tempera colours for colour printing originals. The standard colours for three- and four-colour printing are yellow, cyan, and magenta. These three colours and their first tone subtractive mixtures are obtainable as tempera colours. It is a great help to the blockmaker when you use these special colours.

Casein tempera colours have a pasty consistency. They tend to crack on drying if spread too thickly, so try to use only thin coats of colour. Thin the paint until you can brush it easily. Fluorescent colours are also obtainable. They cannot be mixed with normal colours: their fluorescent effect is destroyed.

Tempera and casein colours dry with a matt finish. To obtain a glossy surface you must use a clear varnish. This can be laid on with a brush or cloth. Spray cans of clear varnish are available, too. Be careful, as varnish alters the colour of the paint. Try the varnish on a colour sample first. You cannot varnish fluorescent colours: their special effect is lost. Remember when using indian inks, that you cannot use ink over tempera or tempera over ink. In both cases the colour will flake off on drying.

Flaking technique

This is a method for producing negative (white-on-black) drawings with a special character. Using tempera white with a little grey mixed in to make the strokes visible, make your brush drawing on well-sized, non-porous paper. When the paint is dry, paint over

Flaking technique. A few drops of thinned white poster colour were scattered by blowing on them

the whole sheet with black indian ink or casein colour. Use a wide brush, and lay on the colour quickly in one coat to avoid dissolving the tempera underneath. As soon as the top coat is dry and shows no more shiny spots, rinse the sheet under running water. The tempera colour will dissolve and wash off, taking its covering of ink or casein colour with it. If the colour is a bit stubborn, help it away a little with a soft brush. The resulting white-on-black drawing has something of the character of a woodcut, with slightly uneven borders.

The same effect can be achieved using rubber solution thinned down with benzine instead of tempera colour. It is difficult to use as it dries quickly and does not flow easily from the brush. On the other hand, it is practical as you can use any kind of colour for the top coat. Water colours are especially good. Finally, when colour and rubber solution are completely dry, rub off the rubber solution with a clean cloth.

Wax crayon work

Many attractive effects can be obtained with oil and wax crayons using different techniques. You can do line drawings or colour flat areas. A light colour laid over a dark one gives a subtractive colour mixture, whereas a dark colour laid over a light one covers it. For instance, blue covers yellow, but yellow over blue gives green. "Sgraffito" technique can be used when several colours are laid over one another. Steel erasers with wooden handles are available, and you may use a needle for the fine work. The crayons can be dissolved in turpentine and brushed evenly over larger areas. You may also shade in the area with crayon and brush on turpentine later.

The water-repellent characteristics of wax can be used to special effect. Make a wax drawing with white crayon and work it with water colour. The water colour will take only where there is no wax on the paper. The result is similar to that of the Javanese "batik" method of dyeing cloths.

You can obtain a similar effect with molten wax. Melt colourless candle wax or stearine in a metal container. You can make a brush drawing with the molten wax. Later, the wax is removed by covering the drawing with a sheet of newspaper and going over it with a hot iron. Again the lines drawn by the wax remain white on the coloured ground. You can make many coloured drawings with this wax technique. When the first drawing is dry, do another detail drawing in wax and paint over again, this time with another colour. Repeat the procedure until your drawing is finished. Start with the lighter colours. The colour mixtures will all be subtractive.

Scraper board technique

Scraper board technique is an interesting method of producing white-and-black drawings. Scraper board consists of a base card coated with white and black chalk layers. The surface layer is scraped with a needle, graver, or blade in a similar way to an etching, exposing the underneath layer. Scraper board can be bought with a white surface and a black underlayer. This gives a black drawing on a white ground. You can make a sort of scraper board of your own by painting over a chalk-coated paper such as poster paper with indian ink. You can then scrape away the black as on proper scraper board.

Recently a method has come into use under the name "photoscrape" process. A light sensitive scraper-board is used on which a half-tone or line image can be created by exposure and developing. The photographic image can then be used as a guide for the artistic use of the scraper. The skilled use of the photoscrape process results in originals for newspaper advertising which have a more striking effect than coarse screen rendering of photographic originals.

Fixing non-permanent colours

When using non-permanent colours, such as charcoal, chalks, and pastels to draw or colour areas with a stump, it is necessary to fix the drawing afterwards. Stumps are small hard rolls of blotting paper.

Pastel drawings are the most difficult to fix successfully. The danger is that the fresh colours may be dulled as the fixative compacts the loosely bound chalk particles together on the paper. When using a mouth spray or a pressurized bottle, do not give the drawing one heavy coat of fixer. This would deaden the colour. Spray several light coats over the drawing, leaving time for each one to dry before the next.

Paste papers

To practise this technique you need wide and narrow brushes, water-soluble colours (tempera is best, but water colours will do), a sheet of glass, and paste (starch paste or cellulose paste). You need a good tough cartridge paper. Lay the paper on the glass sheet and damp it well with a wet sponge. Thin the paste with water and lay on a thin even coat. Brush on the colour over the paste. Carry out your design with a decorator's graining comb or a brush handle, spreading the colour as you want. Lay the finished designs to dry. Many effects are possible with this method. For instance if you mix the colour in with the paste, the results will have a different quality.

Marble papers

To make marble papers you need a large shallow dish such as a photographic bath, a stiff brush, and oil colours. Fill the dish with water. Thin the oil colours with turpentine and drop some colour on to the water surface. The colour will float on the surface and you can stir it into many patterns and shapes. Now lay a sheet of paper on the surface, rolling it on gently from one end. Leave it there for a few seconds and lift it cleanly away. The colours will remain on the paper. To stop the colours making a heavy impression on the surface you may add a measure of size to the water.

To set the colours on the paper more firmly, an adhesive solution is used. A suitable solution may be made with size, or with carragheen moss, which is often used in the trade. The following formula is typical:
1 part carragheen moss
50 parts boiling water
10 parts cold water
Bring the moss to the boil two or three times, take the pot away from the heat and pour in the cold water. Let the mixture cool and sieve it through a linen cloth into the dish. A little ox-gall is added to the special marble effect colours to make them disperse on the base.

It is a good idea to dampen the paper with a weak alum solution to make the colours hold better. You may distribute the colours at will with a brush, comb, or a rod on the base. Take the prints in the same way as oil papers, and lay them out to dry. You can also make marble effects with oil colours and carragheen moss.

Lettering

The lettering on a design, whether it is a poster, an advertisement, a catalogue, or even a printed sheet, is always done last. But it must be planned for at the very beginning. Account must be taken of the size, sort, amount, and position of the type. Lettering is a major part of the design. It can make the design if it is properly integrated, or it can ruin the work if it comes as an afterthought. In the latter case, we must find a make-shift solution, and this is not always satisfactory.

Printing on transparent foil

This is a simple method of lettering a design with printed letters. Determine the size and position of the lettering and get the printer to print an impression on a thin transparent foil. Fix this foil down at the corners over the design; it will give an impression of the finished work. The letters can be printed in any colour, and negative lettering is simply printed white. There is no need to cover large designs completely with the foil. Simply cut out the area round the letters and stick it down with rubber solution. This is usually neat enough for most jobs.

Cut-out letters

You can buy cut-out letters in various sizes, type faces, and colours, but the choice of styles is not very great. Some makes are gummed on the back and can be stuck down directly. It is as well to draw guide lines on the paper to enable you to arrange the letters neatly.

Self-adhesive letters

An extremely easy method of putting lettering on to a drawing is to use letters printed on self-adhesive foil. There is a large range of type faces, numerals, signs, etc., in all common sizes and in various colours. Each sheet contains several examples of each letter, arranged alphabetically on an adhesive-backed transparent foil. The sheet has a protective backing sheet. Cut out the letters you need with a sharp knife, remove them from the backing sheet and stick them down on the design. Press them down lightly with your fingernail. Guide lines are printed under the letters on each sheet to help you arrange the letters evenly. These guide lines are cut off later. You can remove or alter any damaged or falsely positioned letters quite easily.

A design lettered with adhesive characters.
The finished work is even and clean
so that a block can be made from it

It's worth
coming to Paris

A typical sheet of self-adhesive lettering

It is possible to make a block straight from letters "set" in this way.

An even easier method is the "Letraset Instant Lettering" system. This is a direct dry transfer method. An extremely wide range of type sizes in many faces is available not only in European types but also for Oriental and other foreign languages. The selection of types is supplemented by sheets with architectural and engineering symbols, mathematical and electronic signs and other special art or screen designs. The letters can be obtained in black, white and several colours. Each sheet is transparent and has a backing sheet. The letters and numbers are arranged alphabetically. Remove the backing and lay the transparent sheet over the work. Select the letter you need and line it up by the guide line printed on the sheet. Rub across the letter with a hard point such as a pencil or ball pen, using medium pressure. The letter will transfer to the paper, and the sheet is pulled away. Repeat the procedure until the lettering is completed.

Type specimen sheets

Some type foundries publish type specimen sheets for design work. You can cut letters, words, or passages of text out of the sheets and mount them on the work.

Rubber stamps

A rubber stamp set can also be very practical for lettering work. Letters, numerals, signs, and accents are cast in rubber and mounted on wooden bodies rather like enlarged metal types. The body-size is given on each stamp, and so it is possible to calculate the

Letters printed from a rubber stamp.
To produce an even impression, ink the stamp and overprint the letter two or three times.

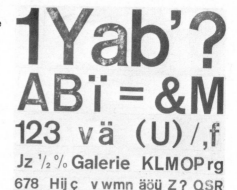

length of set lines exactly. The letters are set in a sort of composing stick, loaded with ink, and pressed on to the paper consecutively. The inks are obtainable in several colours and can be mixed to give a limited number of tones. The ink takes on every sort of surface. Several faces and sizes of type are available.

Drawn letters

You may often find it impossible to use any of the methods described. Either you have not got enough letters, or you cannot get any at all, or the typeface you want is not available to give the necessary impression.

Hand lettering drawn with:
1 A script pen
2 A round-hand pen
3 A brush

¹ match attention
standard

RODIN Clarence
CAESAR ANTINOUS

³ Savanarola
trombone gruff

In such a case you must draw the letters by hand. The letters may be drawn on a sheet of tracing paper, using any method you like, pencil and ruler, a square script pen, or a round script pen. A square pen gives thick and thin strokes and a round pen lines of even thickness. It is best to shade in letters drawn in pencil to give a better idea of the contrast. When you are satisfied with the lettering, trace it through on to your design.

Lay the tracing paper over your work with the lettering in the right position and secure it against movement. Put a sheet of carbon paper underneath the lettering. Now, using a compass and french curve, draw over all the curved parts of the letters first with a hard pencil and medium pressure. Next draw in all the straight lines using a T-square and set-square. When you are finished, remove the tracing and carbon paper, and the outlines of the letters will be left on the work underneath. Now draw in the outlines in paint or ink with a ruling pen and compass, again doing all the curves first to get smooth transitions from straights to curves. Finally fill in the outlines with a brush.

Brush and pen lettering

If the lettering is to be freely written with a pen or brush, you can of course do it directly on the work after one or two practice runs on another sheet. The character of the writing will then remain. You may find your hand becomes unsteady as you realize that you may ruin the almost finished work at one stroke. In this case, it will help to trace the outlines lightly on to the work first. It would be wrong now to set to work to

167

correct all the little irregularities which the finished hand-written letters will inevitably have. This would destroy the very essence of their character.

Trimming the work

The finished work must be trimmed. If you are working on a stretched sheet, first cut it free from the board, and trim the edges later. Remember to allow for the printing border. You must leave about $\frac{1}{8}-\frac{1}{4}$ in. (3–5 mm.) on a design the same size as its eventual reproduction. If the design is to be reduced in size, you must leave proportionately more. Use a steel straightedge and steel square when trimming the work. If you have not got a steel square, draw the edges in accurately first with a tee-square and set-square. Lay something hard under the work to cut on to (a piece of hardboard or aluminium sheet is good). Do not try to cut right through in one go, but press the straightedge down well and make several light cuts.

TECHNICAL DRAWINGS

As a graphic designer you may be faced with the problem of having to do an engineering drawing. A client may require such a drawing of his product or a part of it to appear in the advertising matter you are preparing. The following pages contain a brief explanation of the rules for engineering drawing. This survey is by no means complete. It is intended to give you a basic knowledge sufficient for you to produce drawings which, if they are not one hundred per cent correct, are at least understandable and graphically pleasing. Here again, it is necessary to work cleanly and exactly. You also need good instruments and to know how to use them and, lastly, a little patience.

Instruments

1. *Drawing board.* You will do your work on a drawing board. This must be absolutely flat, and free from knots. One side (or end) should be absolutely true so that the T-square can be used accurately. Good drawing boards are made of pine or spruce.

2. *T-square.* T-squares are made of mahogony or beech, or sometimes of plastic. The T-square should be long enough to reach over the whole drawing board. The T-square is used for drawing horizontal lines on the board. The stock should always be kept tight up against the left-hand edge of the board. Steady the square with your left hand. Lines are ruled with pencil or pen along the top bevelled edge of the tongue.

3. *Set-squares.* Set-squares are made of wood, metal, or plastic. The latter are to be preferred as they last longer and do not warp. There are three main sorts of set-square: 45° squares, 60° squares, and adjustable squares. Each type is obtainable in several sizes. Set-squares are used for drawing vertical and anged lines. Run the set-square along the T-square tonglue and hold it firm with your left hand.

4. *Ruler and straightedge.* Rulers and straightedges are also made of different materials. They are flat strips of wood, metal, or plastic. Usually one edge at least is

bevelled and one or both sides may carry an engraved and coloured scale. Some have one edge specially made for drawing with a ruling pen. The edge is raised to stop the ink running and creeping underneath.

5. *Drawing tables and drawing machines.* Drawing tables are really large drawing boards mounted adjustably on a heavy stand of one type or another. Some have a straightedge mounted on steel wire on a roller system at each side enabling the straightedge to be moved up and down the board. Drawing machines combine all the functions of a T-square and set-square.

6. *Pencils.* You may like to use ordinary wooden pencils, or you may prefer to use adjustable lead-holders. These are pencil-like instruments with a device for clamping a lead firmly. As the lead wears down you can let it out further, or change it for a different grade. In either case always keep a long fine point to the lead. You can buy special sharpeners for both types, and use a small file or sandpaper block to finish the point. Both pencils and separate leads can be obtained in a variety of soft, medium and hard grades.

7. *Drawing instruments.* A set of drawing instruments consists of several pieces packed together in a flat case. Compasses, dividers, and ruling pens are the basic instruments of any set. You can buy a set containing as much as you want or need; the price is the only limit. A large set may have two pairs of compasses, two pairs of dividers, two or three spring bow compasses and dividers, a pump compass, and several ruling pens, in addition to a small screwdriver, and spare leads and points.

Cases of drawing instruments

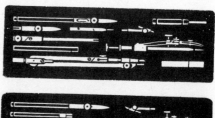

A normal compass consists of two arms hinged together at one end, one carrying a point and the other an attachment for a pen or pencil lead. For large circles an extension piece fits in this arm. Always draw all arcs and circles in pencil first before inking them in.

Dividers are similar to compasses, but each arm has a needle at the end. Dividers are for carrying over dimensions from a ruler or model on to the drawing.

Pump compasses are for drawing very small circles. They have a central pointed shaft around which the pen or lead holder revolves. The pen holder slides up on the shaft so that the point can be placed accurately on the centre. The pen can then be let down on to the paper and turned freely with one finger.

Ruling pens are for drawing in ink. They do not look like normal pens, but have two sharp pointed blades on the end of the handle. An adjustment screw moves the blades nearer or further away from one another to give thin or thick lines. Use a brush or a dropper to load the pen, filling the ink between the blades one drop at a time. Do not get ink on the outside of the blades. One or two drops of ink are enough: too much ink will run out and blot as soon as the pen touches the paper. If the pen will not take, dab it lightly on a damp sponge to moisten the points, which have probably dried. Adjust the pen to give the width of line you want and draw against the edge of a ruler from left to right or from bottom to top. Worn down and blunt pens can be sharpened on a stone. Screw the blades firmly together and grind the pen with a circular movement. The blades must not be too sharp or have rounded points, and must above all be the same length. When the blades are unequal or too sharp the ink will not run from the pen, and if they are too rounded the ink will flow too readily and blot at the end of the lines.

Drawing pens are very practical instruments, like a fountain pen with interchangeable heads. The great advantage is that they need not be continually refilled, and long lines can thus be drawn continuously. Special attachments can be obtained for compass work.

9. *Accessories*: There are various other items that you will find uses for in conjunction with drawing instruments.

Not all curved lines can be drawn with a compass. For these there are many curves available in all sizes and shapes. Normally two or three curves will be enough. The curves are moved around to draw the

171

French curves

lines section by section. A flexible curve, made of soft plastic with a lead and steel-spring core is more practical in many cases. The curve can be bent to the required form and lightly secured with sticky tape.

Lettering may of course be done by hand with a drawing pen, but it is often easier to use a stencil and a special pen. These stencils are positioned with the T-square. Stencils are available with several sizes of both upright and italic lettering. There are special stencils for musical signs, chemical symbols and apparatus, perspective ellipses, and so on.

You must have drawing pins or sticky tape to secure the paper on the board. If you use drawing pins choose ones with rounded heads so the T-square and set-square do not catch as you work. Pin the paper down

Lettering stencil. The letters are cut in a plastic sheet and are drawn with a special pen

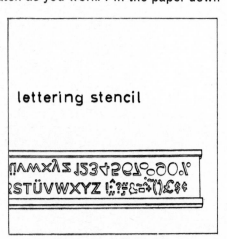

at the corners. You may prefer to use sticky tape, especially if you have a plastic covered drawing board and do not want to damage it with pins.

Pencil marks can be removed with an indiarubber. A soft rubber will do for drawings made with a soft pencil, but for harder leads you must use a hard rubber. Hard rubbers contain fine sand. Ink lines must be scratched out with a razor blade or better with a glass eraser. When using a razor blade, hold the blade at right-angles to the paper and scratch lightly over the mark. Glass fibres should not protrude more than about $\frac{1}{16}$ in. (1–2 cm.) out of the holder. Stretch the paper between two fingers and rub in the direction of the line. Clean up the area afterwards with a soft rubber, and then smooth out any roughness with thumbnail or bone. Should the ink run on the erased area, shade

Erasing stencil to protect the work while erasing detail

in the place with a soft pencil and then draw the line in ink. Finally clean off the pencil with a soft rubber.

Use an erasing stencil when removing details such as single letters in a word or small circles. Erasing stencils are thin sheets of steel with a variety of holes. Lay the stencil with a suitable hole over the unwanted detail to protect the surrounding parts, and simply rub through the hole with the rubber or glass eraser.

Drawing materials

1. *Drawing paper and card*. Drawing paper comes in sheets or rolls. Choose a rough paper for pencil work and a smooth one for ink drawings. You must use a high-quality paper for good results. The best papers

are made of cellulose and rags. They are sized on both sides to give a good drawing surface. Papers backed with linen are obtainable for drawings which must be durable, and there are cards with a core of aluminium foil for jobs where dimensional stability is required. On a good paper the ink should not run and you should be able to redraw lines over erased areas. The paper must also be tough, waterproof and should not fade.

2. *Tracing paper.* Drawings on transparent material are generally duplicated by a photo-copying process. Dye-line printing with dry development, and other direct copying methods are used to give dimensionally accurate reproductions of the original, which must be drawn on tracing cloth or transparent paper. There are several grades of tracing paper differing in thickness, surface finish, and tone. Detail papers are thinner and are used for delicate drawings.

There are also several makes of plastic foil for drawing office use. They are matt on one side and have the advantage that they are dimensionally stable.

Reproduction scales

All drawings should be drawn to scale, and this scale must be indicated on the sheet. Large objects must of course be drawn to a reduced scale to get them on the paper, and small objects or details are usually drawn to a large scale for ease of reading and dimensioning. The following scales are recommended by the British Standards Institution (BS 308):

Recommended Reproduction Scales

Relative sizes	Scale	Relative sizes	Scale
Full size	1 : 1	$\frac{1}{2}$ in.=1 ft.	1 : 24
Half size	1 : 2	$\frac{3}{8}$ in.=1 ft.	1 : 32
3 in.=1 ft.	1 : 4	$\frac{1}{4}$ in.=1 ft.	1 : 48
1$\frac{1}{2}$ in.=1 ft.	1 : 8	$\frac{1}{8}$ in.=1 ft.	1 : 96
1 in.=1 ft.	1 : 12	$\frac{1}{16}$ in.=1 ft.	1 : 192
$\frac{3}{4}$ in.=1 ft.	1 : 16		

The enlargement factors recommended are 2, 4, 8, and 10. The scale must be indicated on the drawing: e.g., Scale 2 : 1. Should it be necessary to use two scales on the same sheet, both must be clearly indicated.

Types of line

The following types of lines should be used for technical drawing:

Thick continuous lines are used for all visible outlines. Keep to the same line thickness right through
the drawing.

Thin continuous lines are for all dimension lines,
projection or extension lines, hatching or sectioning,
and leader lines for notes. Thin lines should be about
a third to half the thickness of the thick lines.

Thin broken lines or dashes are used to show hidden
details or parts to be removed. The dashes should be
about $\frac{1}{8}$ in. (2–3 mm.) long, and the spaces a little
shorter. The line has the same thickness as the thin
continuous lines.

Thin long-chain lines are used for centre lines and
path lines indicating movement. Centre lines should
project for a short distance beyond the outline to
which they refer, but may be extended further to aid
dimensioning or to correlate views.

Thick long chain lines are used for cutting or viewing
planes. The longer dashes should be about $\frac{1}{2}$ in.
(12 mm.) long and the short dashes and spaces about
$\frac{1}{8}$ in. (2–3 mm.) long. When two chain lines cross, they
must do so at two long dashes.

Thin short chain lines are for showing developed
views and adjacent parts.

Thick continuous wavy lines show irregular boundary
lines and short break lines. Often it is not possible or
necessary to show the whole of an object, and the part
cut off is bounded by a wavy line. The line thickness is
the same as for thick continuous lines.

Ruled line with short zig-zags are used for longbreak
lines.

Types of line for technical drawing:
1 Thick continuous
2 Thin continuous
3 Thin broken
4 Thin long-chain
5 Thick long-chain
6 Thin short-chain
7 Thick continuous wavy
8 Ruled short zig-zag

Section lining (*hatching*) consists of thin diagonal parallel lines and is used to indicate cut or broken surfaces. These lines have the same thickness as thin continuous lines. Section lining is usually drawn at 45° to the edges of the sheet, but if the shape or position of the section would bring the section lining nearly parallel to one of the sides another angle may be chosen. The sectioning must be consistent in any one part. Adjacent parts are sectioned in different directions or to a different pitch. Try to avoid dimensions on a sectioned area. Where this is necessary, the section lines should be interrupted.

Dimensioning

All the dimensions necessary for the finishing of the product must be indicated on the drawing. Dimensions should be placed outside the outline, wherever possible. Projection lines, thin full lines projected from the points, lines, or surfaces to be dimensioned, are used for this purpose. Where projection lines are used as an extension of the outline they should start just clear of the outline and extend a little way beyond the dimension lines. Where they refer to intersections or points on a surface, they should touch or pass through these points. In this case the points may be emphasized with small dots.

Dimension lines are thin full lines and have a narrow arrowhead at each end. The arrowheads should be about $\frac{1}{8}$ in. (2–3 mm.) long and should touch the outline or projection line at both ends of the dimension line. Dimensions are normally placed so that they can be

Dimensioning a part (plan, side and end elevations)

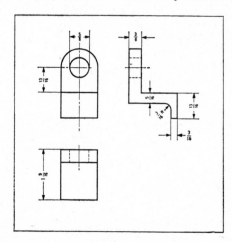

Break lines for rectangular-sectional
subjects are drawn with a continuous wavy
line. The broken ends of a round section
are drawn in a figure-of-eight form
with section lining

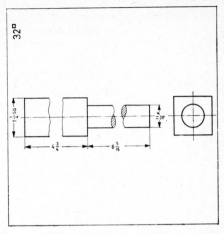

read from the bottom or from the right-hand side of the
drawing. Lines may be broken for the insertion of dimensions. Never use a centre line, an extension of a
centre line, or part of the outline as a dimension line.

Angular dimensions are given in degrees and minutes,
or degrees, minutes, and seconds. The units should
always be clearly indicated. The dimension lines for
angles are drawn as arcs of a circle and the projection
lines are extensions of the angle.

Chordal dimensions are shown by straight lines. An
arc drawn from the same centre is used for *circumferential dimensions*.

Radii are dimensioned by a line through or in line
with the centre of the arc. The dimension line has only
one arrowhead, touching the arc. The diameter and not
the radius should be given for circles.

Dimensioning curved subjects:
1 Angular dimensioning
2 Chordal dimensions
3 Circumferential dimensions

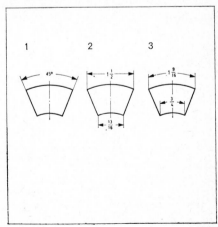

Arrangement of dimensions

The dimension is normally in the middle of the dimension line either above it or in line with it. Sometimes the dimensions may be staggered to avoid confusion with other dimensions or lines. The numbers must be placed to be read from the bottom or the right-hand side of the drawing.

Drawings may be lettered by hand or with a stencil. The letters must be legible and uniform. Sloping or vertical letters are suitable for general use, but always use vertical letters for drawing numbers, titles, and reference numbers. The size of the lettering will depend on the drawing, but it should never be smaller than about $\frac{1}{8}$ in. (2–3 mm.). The standard method of dimensioning is in inches, or in feet and inches. Use only inches for measurements up to 2 ft. The millimetre is the standard unit for metric drawings.

Where two types of unit are used on the same drawing, a prominent note should be added as explanation.

Systems of projection

Two systems of projection, called first-angle and third-angle, are acceptable as standard. In first-angle projection each view shows what would be seen by looking on the far side of the adjacent view. This means that the plan is under the front elevation, and the end elevations are at either side.

In third-angle projection each view shows what would be seen by looking on the near side of the adjacent view. The plan comes above the front eleva-

Arrangement of the views in first-angle projection:
1 Front elevation
2 Side elevation
3 Plan

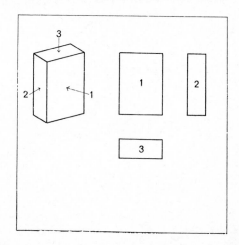

178

Arrangement of the views in third-angle projection:
1 Front elevation
2 Side elevation
3 Plan

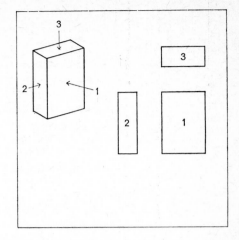

Sectional view:
1 Assembly viewed normally
2 Assembly shown in section

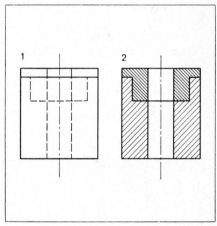

Conventional representation of a bolt with nut (plan and elevation with section)

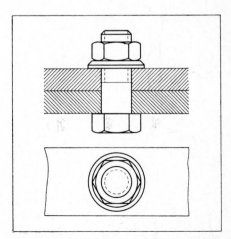

tion, and the end elevations are at the opposite sides to first-angle projection.

Sectional views

Sectional views may be included on the main drawing. The cutting plane is shown by a thick chain line and if necessary the viewing direction is given too. Symmetrical objects may be drawn with one half in outside view and one side in section. Part sections are sometimes needed to show details which would otherwise be hidden. In this case show the boundary of the section with an irregular boundary line.

Perspective projections

It is sometimes helpful to include a perspective view in a drawing, especially when the objects have been drawn larger than full size. An unpractised eye will be able to read and understand the drawing much more easily with the help of a perspective. Parallel perspectives are the easiest to draw, and the views are normally taken from left or right. All the lines which are parallel on the object remain parallel on the drawing, and vertical lines remain vertical. This gives an unusual look to the drawings, but has the advantage that measurements may be taken from the drawing.

There are two main types of perspective projection:

1. *Dimetric projection.* The plan of the object forms the basis of the drawing. With a right-angled plan, draw lines in one direction at an angle of 7° to the horizontal with their full length. Shorten lines at right-angles to half their length and draw them at 42° to the horizontal. Vertical lines retain their normal size.

A subject shown in dimetric projection

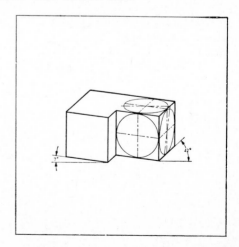

A subject shown in isometric projection

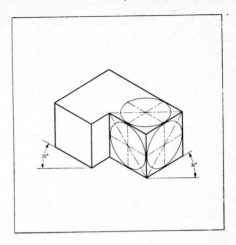

2. *Isometric projection.* All lines retain their normal projections in isometric projection. Horizontal lines at right-angles to one another are drawn at 30° to the horizontal. The verticals remain vertical. The front and rear edges of a cube drawn in isometric projection are in line with one another. This sometimes confuses the drawing.

MATERIALS

As a graphic designer, you should know the materials which will concern you during the designing and printing of your designs. Only then will you be able to choose the best materials for the work and make the best use of them. Paper is essential for all graphic design work, but inks, paint, varnishes, glues, and many other materials play their part in determining the success or failure of the final design.

Paper

The choice of paper is extremely important for the success of a printing project. It is certain, too, that the quality of the paper plays an important part. The right paper brings out the full effect of good printing, and increases the intrinsic value of the work. It should be a delight to look at the finished page, and an aesthetic delight to finger it. The beauty of the paper should not be hidden under a mass of printing: wide margins and spaces should remain to let the paper speak for itself.

There are several kinds of paper: rag paper, wood pulp paper, and "wood-free" paper. Rag paper contains only cloth fibres such as linen, cotton, or hemp. Rag paper is considered the best quality paper and is used for valuable documents and as high quality drawing paper.

Paper with a maximum of 50 per cent wood pulp in bleached or unbleached cellulose fibres is said to be wood-free paper. Cellulose pulp is obtained from wood or other vegetable material by chemical treatment, for instance with caustic soda or sulphite liquor.

Wood pulp papers contain more than 5 per cent wood pulp. For instance, newsprint consists of 85–90 per cent wood pulp. This wood pulp is produced by mechanical means, such as shredding or grinding. Such papers are rough and brittle and are used for newspaper printing or as packing papers and so on. Papers are differentiated according to their wood content: normal printing paper with 75 per cent wood pulp and 25 per cent cellulose pulp, medium paper with

70 per cent wood pulp and 30 per cent cellulose pulp, and fine paper with 60 per cent wood pulp and 40 per cent cellulose pulp.

The raw material, wood pulp, cellulose pulp, and perhaps paper scrap, is first crushed in a beating mill, and mixed with size, alum, and filler. The resulting "stuff" or "stock" now flows over a riffle, or sand trap and into the pulp strainer. The sand trap is a trough with laths placed across the bottom. The pulp strainer holds back clumps of pulp and large pieces of wood. The pulp then flows on to the endless wire mesh sieve of the machine. The rate of supply and the speed of the sieve band can be altered to obtain any thickness of ply. The wire mesh oscillates to and fro at one end so that the fibres felt together and orientate themselves in

Elements of a paper-making machine:

1 Pulp strainer
2 Wire mesh belt
3 Couch and press roller
4 Drying end
5 Calender
6 Paper roll

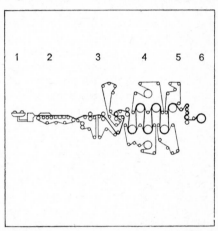

the direction of flow. A large amount of the water content drips out through the mesh, and still more is pressed out of the web by heated rollers. The web is finally dried between further rollers and leaves the machine as machine-finished (M.F.) paper. Sometimes the paper goes through a "super-calender" to obtain a smoother surface and higher gloss. It is then known as "supercalendered paper".

The extent of pulverization in the beating mill determines the quality (and thus to some extent, the use) of the paper. There are various different grades of fibres: free-beaten coarse, long (blotting papers, filter papers); coarse, short (lightweight papers, printing papers); wet-beaten, long (imitation parchment, tracing paper, bank-note paper); wet-beaten, short (writing paper).

The different grades are achieved by resetting the cutters of the pulping machine and varying the pulping time. Short, sharp pulping produces coarse, free-beaten pulp. During longer pulping under light pressure the pulp is not cut up, but evenly squashed so that the individual fibres are separated. These fine fibres felt together very strongly and closely, giving a tough paper.

Machine direction

The machine direction (or making direction) plays an important part for the printer and bookbinder. The pulp fibres orientate themselves mainly parallel to the flow direction of the mesh of the paper mill. The finished paper comes off the machine in a continuous strip and usually leaves the factory in rolls. If the paper is despatched in sheets, the machine direction is usually given on the package.

Sheets are called wide roll or narrow roll. In the first case, individual sheets are cut from the roll so that the height of the paper is the width of the roll. In the second, the width of the paper is the same as that of the roll. In wide roll sheets, then, the fibres run at right-angles to the long sides, and in narrow roll sheets parallel to the long sides. These differences become very important later, during printing.

The fibres of the paper should run through the printing press parallel to the roller. The paper is expanded evenly and the adjustments for register of the second impression are made easier. Creases may arise when no account is taken of the machine direction. The book-

Machine direction is different on wide roll
sheets and narrow roll sheets:
1 Wide roll
2 Narrow roll

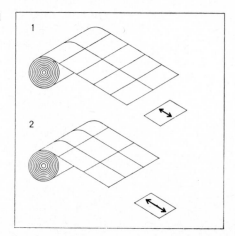

binder, too, must take care. The machine direction must be parallel to the binding, or the pages will cockle at the slightest sign of moisture.

Determining machine direction

The machine direction is usually given on the package, or can be seen on the surface of the paper. If not, one of the following methods may be used:

1. *Tearing test* (*for thin paper*). Tear a little way into the sheet, from the long side and from the short side. The straighter tear will be along the machine direction.
2. *Fingernail test* (*for medium papers*). Pull two adjacent edges of a sheet between your first finger and thumb in two directions. One edge will buckle more than the other. The machine direction runs at right-angles to this edge.

Tests to determine machine direction:

1 Tearing

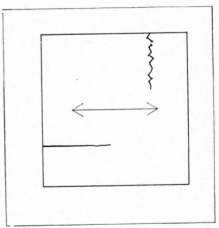

2 Fingernail

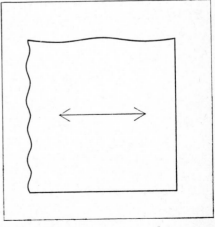

3 Bending

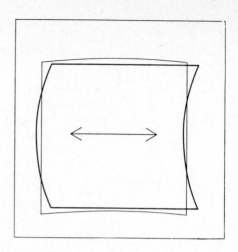

3. *Bending test* (*for heavy papers and card*). Cut a piece of paper the size of a playing card out of the sheet. Span the paper in your hand and bend it gently in two direc- tions. The paper will bend more easily in one direction. The machine direction runs parallel to this bend.
4. *Dampness test*. Damp one side of a small sheet and lay it, damp side down, on the flat of your hand. It will curl up in one direction, parallel to the machine direction. In cases of doubt, this method is the surest. It works for almost any paper, apart from very porous types like blotting and filter papers.
5. *Charring test*. With heavy card it is also necessary to see whether the board has been couched or laminated from thin sheets of poor quality paper. Couched paper

4 Dampness

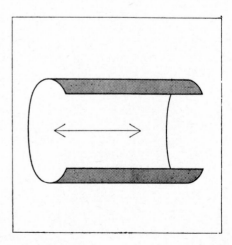

5 Charring

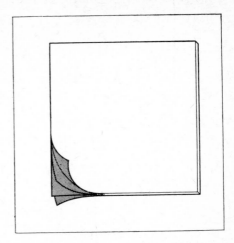

consists of several layers felted together during manufacture. Hold a flame to the corner of a sheet until it begins to char. A couched paper chars evenly away, whereas a laminated sheet separates into clearly recognizable layers.

Paper in printing

There is a noticeable difference between the two sides of machine-finished (M.F.) paper. The face of the paper which lay on the wire mesh during manufacture is called the wire side. The other face is called the top side. Half-tones are printed on the top side whenever possible. Supercalendered paper (S.C.), sometimes called imitation art paper, is paper which has been through a supercalender, where some of the rollers are of compressed fibre and some of metal. It has a much smoother, glossier surface, and can take half-tone blocks down to 120–133 screen, depending on the degree of supercalendering. It is thus suitable for the simpler printing processes. Blocks with screens down to 85 can be printed successfully for magazines and catalogues. These papers are called uncoated papers, as distinct from the coated papers, or art papers.

The finest half-tone screens, well printed on art paper, give excellent results. Art papers are coated with a mineral substance such as china clay or blanc fixe with an adhesive such as casein. The pores between the fibres of the paper are filled by the coating to provide a smoother and whiter surface. Wood pulp and wood free papers are given an elastic, porous surface. Art papers are coated on both sides. Chromo papers, coated on one side only, are used for packages and such. Colouring matter may also be mixed into the filter to produce coloured art paper.

The printer checks the quality of the paper before starting work. The paper must not crack or give off dust. Paper may have been badly sized or have been too dryly stored. During the printing the filler then begins to fall out of the paper and blocks the spaces of the letters and blocks. This gives a dirty looking impression. By tapping and rubbing together two sheets of paper over a black surface, the printer can see whether the paper dusts a lot or a little.

Sometimes, when the paper has been badly coated, the sticky printing ink on the type pulls off the coated surface of the paper with it. This is called plucking. Sometimes it even pulls fibres out of the paper. This is called picking. It can be cured by thinning the ink a little. The printer tests the paper by taking a little ink on his finger and dabbing it on the paper repeatedly. When the surface withstands 10–20 dabs, the paper can be considered strong enough.

Sizing

Papers are classified according to their amount of size into: unsized, 1/4, 1/2, 3/4, 1/1, and hard sized. You cannot erase on surface-sized boards: after several passes the surface is destroyed and the ink blots. Drawing papers, writing papers, and illumination or lettering papers are sized right through. Very good drawing papers are sized again on the surface with an animal size.

Embossing and watermarking

Embossing is carried out by special overlays on the wire mesh or in a special embossing press. The rollers of the embossing press are clad with various surfaced lines to give a variety of paper effects such as hammered paper, linen paper, and ribbed paper. Watermarks are introduced into the paper in the machine. A wire image is attached to the surface of a roller, under which the wet paper is pressed. The wire compresses the paper locally, and it becomes translucent.

Shaded watermarks are produced in the moist paper by raised and recessed patterns on the wire mesh. At the raised bits the ply becomes thinner and more transparent, and at the recessed bits thicker and more opaque. This gives the characteristic soft transitions from light to dark, as distinct from the hard lines of

Examples of watermarks

normal watermarks. Shaded watermarks are extremely difficult to copy and are used for money notes and important documents. Imitation watermarks are obtained by pressing an image into the finished paper. Sometimes a colourless fatty ink is printed on to the paper. This makes the image transparent and gives the appearance of a watermark.

Packing papers and boards

Cheap papers, used for packing papers, wrapping papers, paper bags and carriers, are made of straw and brown wood pulp and even waste paper pulp. Strawpaper can be recognized by its generally yellow colour, and waste paper board by its grey tone. Yellow straw paper and board is the cheapest paper and is stiff and brittle. The grey-white board is also brittle but is often used by bookbinders for mounting thin white paper or stiffening books and folders. Leatherpulp board contains not less than 50 per cent leather pulp and is very tough. It is used for making folders and packing cases.

In addition to solid board, corrugated board is often used for packaging consisting of a lamination of thin corrugated material and one or two thin plain boards. For equal stiffness corrugated board is very much lighter than plain board.

Standard paper sizes

There are several basic sizes of paper, which are cut to give a range of different sheets. To find what basic size a sheet has come from you must multiply by two, four, and so on as the case may be.

Basic Paper Sizes

Name	Size in inches	Area in sq. inches
Imperial	22×30	660
Large Royal	$20\frac{1}{2} \times 27$	$553\frac{1}{2}$
Elephant	20×27	540
Royal	20×25	500
Small Royal	19×24	456
Medium	18×23	414
Demy	$17\frac{1}{2} \times 22\frac{1}{2}$	$393\frac{3}{4}$
Large Post	$16\frac{1}{2} \times 21$	$346\frac{1}{2}$
Small Demy	$15\frac{1}{2} \times 20$	310
Crown	15×20	300
Post	15×1	285
Foolscap	$13\frac{1}{2} \times 17$	$228\frac{1}{2}$
Small Foolscap	$13\frac{1}{4} \times 16\frac{1}{2}$	$218\frac{5}{8}$

The sheet can be cut or folded into two, four, six, etc., sheets. It is then known by the name of its basic size. followed by the fold or cut (folio, quarto, octavo, etc.)

Royal Sheet Division

Division	Size in inches	Division	Size in inches
Folio	$12\frac{1}{2} \times 20$	9mo	$6\frac{2}{3} \times 8\frac{1}{3}$
4to	$10 \times 12\frac{1}{2}$	12mo	$6\frac{1}{4} \times 6\frac{2}{3}$
Long 4to	$6\frac{1}{4} \times 20$	Long 12mo	$5 \times 8\frac{1}{3}$
6mo.	$8\frac{1}{3} \times 10$	16mo	$5 \times 6\frac{1}{4}$
Long 6mo	$6\frac{2}{3} \times 12\frac{1}{2}$	24mo	$4\frac{1}{8} \times 5$
8vo	$6\frac{1}{4} \times 10$	32mo	$3\frac{1}{8} \times 5$
Long 8vo	$5 \times 12\frac{1}{2}$		

Thus, a Royal octavo page would be $6\frac{1}{4} \times 10$ in.

ISO paper sizes

For some time there has been a growing interest in the United Kingdom in the ISO A and B (metric) sizes of paper and certain of them are being used by a number of organizations. The principal advantage of the system on which these sizes are based is that every size in the main and subsidiary ranges has the same proportions. This facilitates enlargement or reduction of printed matter, diagrams and similar material by photographic means.

The sizes of the principal and subsidiary series are designated by the letters A or B indicating the series, and a number which indicates how many times the basic size of the series (known as 0) has to be divided to produce them.

Construction of the 150 sheet size. The basic sheet AO has an area of 1 sq. metre. The proportion of the short side to the long side is that of the side of a square to it diagonal = a : d = 1 : 1.414 or 5 : 7

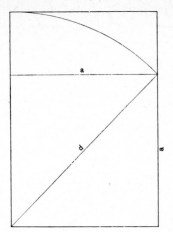

Halving any 150 sheet gives the next smaller size. The number indicates how many times the basic sheet has been folded

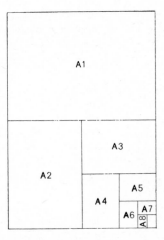

ISO "A" Series

Trimmed size

Designation	mm.	inches
A0	841 × 1189	33·11 × 46·81
A1	594 × 841	23·39 × 33·11
A2	420 × 594	16·54 × 23·39
A3	297 × 420	11·69 × 16·54
A4	210 × 297	8·27 × 11·69
A5	148 × 210	5·83 × 8·27
A6	105 × 148	4·13 × 5·83
A7	74 × 105	2·91 × 4·13
A8	52 × 74	2·05 × 2·91

The sizes of the B series are intended for use only in exceptional circumstances when sizes are needed intermediate between any two adjacent sizes of the A

191

150 folder size (99 × 210 mm) based on
the A1 sheet

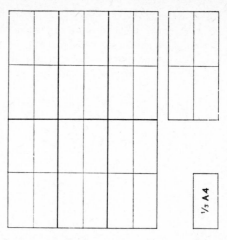

series. When such circumstances arise, they may be
used for the same purposes as those mentioned for
the A series.

ISO "B" Series

Designation	mm.	inches
	Trimmed size	
B0	1000 × 1414	39·37 × 55·67
B1	707 × 1000	27·83 × 39·37
B2	500 × 707	19·68 × 27·83
B3	353 × 500	13·90 × 19·68
B4	250 × 353	9·84 × 13·90
B5	176 × 250	6·93 × 9·84
B6	125 × 176	4·92 × 6·93
B7	88 × 125	3·46 × 4·92
B8	62 × 88	2·44 × 3·46

Long Sizes

Designation	mm.	inches
	Trimmed size	
1·3 A4	99 × 210	3·90 × 8·27
1·4 A4	74 × 210	2·91 × 8·27

The long sizes are intended for use for labels, tickets
and similar products. They should in practice be
produced from the A series only.

Paper weight

The conventional way of giving paper weights is in
pounds per 500 sheets. This is gradually being replaced
by the international method of grammes per square
metre. The thickness of the paper can be deduced
from the weight, for instance a metre square sheet of

80 g/m² is 0·08 mm. thick. It is useful to know the weights of the various standard sizes to compare weights of different sizes of the same paper. Use the following formula:

$$\frac{W \times A \times B}{C \times D} = x \text{ lb.}$$

W   =weight of paper known
A×B=size of paper required
C×D=size of paper of known weight

The following list shows some sample sizes and weights of some of the more important kinds of paper.

COATED PAPERS
Super Coated Art
Cast Coated: s/o Double Crown 36–57 gsm 85–135
Chromo: s/o Double Crown 34–72 gsm 79–169
Coated Art
Esparto brush-coated art:
             s/o Double Crown 42–80 gsm 98–190
Creamy and toned esparto brush-coated art:
             s/o Double Crown 45–60 gsm 105–142
Wood-free brush-coated art:
             s/o Double Crown 45–60 gsm 105–142
Offset machine-coated art:
             s/o Double Crown 36–60 gsm 84–142
Machine Coated Art
Esparto machine-coated art:
             s/o Double Crown 36–50 gsm 85–118
Woodfree machine-coated art:
             s/o Double Crown 36–60 gsm 85–142
Mechanical machine-coated art:
             s/o Double Crown 27–45 gsm 63–105

UNCOATED PAPERS
Antique
Esparto antique: s/o Double Crown 35–60 gsm 79–142
Mechanical antique:
             s/o Double Crown 35–60 gsm 79–142
Cartridge
Esparto offset cartridge:
             s/o Double Crown 38–60 gsm 107–143
Special furnish offset cartridge:
             s/o Double Crown 36–58 gsm 85–136
Wood-free offset cartridge:
             s/o Double Crown 40–58 gsm 94–136
Imitation Art
Imitation art: s/o Double Crown 36–50 gsm 85–118

Super Calendered
Wood-free S.C.: s/o Double Crown 24–45 gsm 56–105
Special furnish S.C.:
　　　　　　　s/o Double Crown 45–58 gsm 105–130
Mechanical S.C.: s/o Double Crown 25–36 gsm 58–84
Machine Finished
Esparto M.F.:　　s/o Double Crown 24–60 gsm 56–143
Wood-free M.F.: s/o Double Crown 24–40 gsm 56–94
Mechanical M.F.: s/o Double Crown 27–58 gsm 63–136
Tinted papers (coloured)
Tinted printing: s/o Double Crown 25–63 gsm 58–143
M.G. Poster (packaging and poster)
M.G. Poster:　　s/o Double Crown 22–40 gsm 51–93
The weights represent the heaviest and lightest available, there being many weights between. "S/o Double Crown"=substance of Double Crown (20×30 in.). This is the English method of describing and comparing different weights of paper.

Types of paper

The following is a list of the main sorts of paper and their trade names in alphabetical order. It contains a short description of the characteristics and uses of each paper.

AIR-MAIL. A very light paper similar in characteristics to thin typewriter paper.

ART. Mostly wood-free paper, coated on both sides and heavily calendered. Art paper is obtainable with matt, semi-matt, or glossy surface finish. It is suitable for printing with the finest half-tone screens as well as with offset and intaglio. Two-coloured art papers are also obtainable (mostly white on one side and coloured on the other, or coloured on both sides). This colouring often saves colour printing. Art paper can be folded and stamped well.

BANK, see WRITING.

BIBLE PRINTING. A high-quality lightweight paper, usually containing rag, used for printing large works whose volume must be kept down. It is also used for printing Bibles and prayer books.

BLOTTING. Fibrous paper which is very porous.

BOND. A tough writing paper for use in typewriters. Translucent varieties are obtainable for dye-line printing.

BULK, see ESPARTO.

BOX ENAMEL. A paper similar to chromo paper, but with a waterproof coating. It is used for making all sorts of packages and bookjackets. Coloured box enamel papers are obtainable.

CAST-COATED PAPER AND BOARD. Paper coated on one or both sides with a mirror-like surface calendered on heated, chromium-plated rollers. It has an appearance like Cellophaned paper when printed with glossy inks, and is suitable for the finest half-tone screens.

CHROMO PAPER AND BOARD. Mostly wood-free paper, coated on one side. It is suitable for covering packages. The surface is similar to art paper. Chromo board must be suitable for folding and scoring and is used for packages.

CIGARETTE. A paper similar to tissue paper.

DRAWING. High quality rag paper and board with an animal glue surface coating, withstanding erazing. Obtainable with rough or smooth surfaces. Drawing papers for school use usually contain wood and are of generally poorer quality.

DUPLICATING. Lightly sized wood paper used for duplicating in office machines.

ENVELOPE. Made in all grades and usually glossy on one side only. The paper must be very tough to withstand the rigours of the post.

ESPARTO. Also known as bulk paper or featherweight paper. The best qualities are wood-free, but it is normally a wood paper. It can be printed well. It has a soft, thick feel and is used for adding bulk to works.

FEATHERWEIGHT, see ESPARTO

GRAVURE. A soft, porous paper. It must be soft and flexible for intaglio printing.

HAND OR MOULD MADE. Paper made in single sheets by hand, characterized by deckle edges. The name has been debased, as "hand-made" papers are usually machine made nowadays.

HARD-SIZED PRINTING. A wood paper used for pre-printing forms. It takes ink and can be used in typewriters.

IMITATION ART. A general term for wood-free papers loaded with a suitable filler and well calendered. Half-tone blocks can be printed on imitation art paper, up to 120 lines on the better, smoother qualities.

IMITATION GREASE-PROOF. Paper thinner than parchment paper with a high gloss obtained by moistening and subsequent hot calendering.

IMPREGNATED. Paraffin or wax papers, waterproof papers, fire-proof papers are all impregnated papers.

195

They all receive a special surface treatment, and are used for food packages, overseas parcels, etc. They are gradually being ousted by plastic-coated papers.

INDEX PAPER AND BOARD. Best quality wood-free paper and board, usually coloured or ruled. It takes ink and can be used in a typewriter. When used for index cards, the machine direction must be vertical so that the cards do not warp.

IVORY BOARD. Highest quality board with alabaster-like surface. It has good printing, embossing, and scoring characteristics and is suitable for greeting cards, visiting cards, and the like.

JAPANESE. Papers made by hand from mulberry fibres.

LEDGER. Well-sized writing paper for office and similar use. It is made from rag with cellulose additive.

LETTERPRESS. This is a general term for machine-glazed wood or wood-free papers used for pocket books, labels, advertising sheets and other similar short-lived articles.

MACHINE-COATED. These papers are not coated on special coating machines like art papers, but direct in the paper machine. They are much whiter than un-coated papers. Despite the fact that their surface is never as good as the absolutely closed, high gloss finish of art papers, machine-coated papers can be printed with half-tone screens as fine as 133.

MANILA. A tough wood-free paper or card used mainly for punched cards or packages.

MECHANICAL WRAPPING. Brown paper made with brown mechanical wood pulp.

NEEDLE. Packing papers free from chlorine, acids, and alkalis. They are also known as "rust protective papers" and are used for packing bright metal parts.

NEWSPRINT. A cheap mechanical wood machine-glazed paper for newspaper printing. It is very lightly sized and can only be printed with coarse half-tone blocks.

OFFSET. Offset papers are well-sized wood or wood-free papers. The surface is machine-glazed or rough. Papers for rotary offset magazine work are very woody.

PARCHMENT. Grease-proof paper made by wet beating the long fibres.

PART MECHANICAL SUPER-CALENDERED PRINT-ING. This is a well-calendered wood-pulp paper which can be printed with relatively fine half-tone screens.

PASTEBOARD. A lamination of a woody base with

two wood-free card faces. Sometimes wrongly called Bristol board.

SECURITY. A fine paper of highest quality for bank notes, shares, and cheques.

SQUARED, LINED, GRAPH. Paper printed with squares or lines for making graphs, or for use in exercise books, etc.

SURFACED. These are papers treated with plastic and used for packages and the like.

SYNTHETIC. These are made with synthetic fibres and have special characteristics such as high mechanical strength or dimensional stability. They can hardly be torn and are very durable. They are suitable for a wide range of printing processes, especially offset. They have a surface like offset papers, and will take writing, are washable and will withstand hot water. The most frequent uses are: identification papers, documents, advertising matter, instruction cards, filing cards, and dimensionally stable drawings.

TISSUE. A very thin, semi-transparent paper. Coloured tissue papers are also available.

WATERPROOF, see IMPREGNATED, SURFACED.

WAXED, see IMPREGNATED.

WRAPPING. There are several kinds of wrapping paper: white and brown, unglazed and machine glazed on one or both sides; mechanical papers made from wood pulp, as well as from rags and from scrap paper; yellow straw papers, which are the poorest quality and are usually made into corrugated paper. Bags and carriers are made of good quality wrapping paper on a bag glueing machine. Crêpe papers are crinkled across the roll by a special cylinder in the paper machine while still wet.

WRITING. This may be any well-sized rough calendered or machine-glazed paper from wood pulp to wood free and 100 per cent rag papers. Ink does not run on them, and they will withstand erasing. The different sorts of writing paper are: bond, airmail, concept, typewriter, envelope, ledger, and bank. Letter papers and bank papers are made not only in white, but in various colours.

Adhesives and size

The basic types are animal and vegetable glues, which are marketed under a wide range of trade and brand names.

197

Animal glues

Hide and bone glues are made from animal skins and bones by chemical treatment and heating in water to extract the protein which sets to form a stiff jelly on cooling. Glues are used as adhesives and as binders for pigments. They can be bought in blocks or granules. The granules are made by dropping molten glue into benzine, where it solidifies immediately into drops. One type of bone glue has chalk powder added. Gelatine is a refined form of glue; it is mostly made from the tissues of calves and sheep. Fish glue is made from fish waste.

Skin glues are mostly light coloured and transparent, whereas bone glues are darker. They are both soluble in warm water. They can be used as binders with every kind of pigment but are not water- and weatherproof when dry. However, they can be emulsified with various oil-base binders and can be mixed with other kinds of glue including synthetic resin glues (see page 197). Bone and skin glues are used primarily in the bookbinding and packaging trades.

Casein glues

Casein is a protein of milk available in powder form. As such it is not soluble in water. To make it soluble it must be chemically treated with lime to form lime-casein, or with an alkali such as caustic soda, borax, sodium carbonate, or liquid ammonia to convert it to a casein alkali. The lime-casein glues are used for woodwork, and only the alkali caseins are suitable for use as binders. They are compatible with all pigments, and can be emulsified with oil bases or mixed with other glues. Casein colours are waterproof, and to a large extent weatherproof on a good surface.

Vegetable adhesives

1. *Starch paste.* Starch is obtained from potatoes, wheat-, rye-, rice-, or maize-flour. Commercially, these raw materials are mixed with water, heated, and treated with caustic soda to release the starch. The mixture is then dried between heated rollers to produce the starch-paste powder.

   You can make starch paste yourself by brewing the raw materials in hot water, but this gives a paste with reduced adhesive properties. Mix the starch with an equal quantity of cold water and then add ten parts boiling water.

Starch paste can be mixed with other adhesives and can be emulsified with oil-bases and synthetic resins. It is used mainly as a wallpaper glue and as size. It has a glazing effect and is used in preparing coated paper.

2. *Dextrin*. Dextrin is obtained by decomposing potato or maize starch under the influence of dilute nitric acid and heat. After being dried, it is roasted at about 175–320°F (80–100°C). The yellowish-white powder is dissolved in hot water before use. Dextrin is used for sticking labels, postage stamps, and envelopes. As a binder it is used mostly for water-colours. Dextrin is especially good for stretching large sheets of paper.

3. *Cellulose glue*. Cellulose glue is produced by converting insoluble cellulose into soluble cellulose compounds. Treatment with caustic soda produces soda cellulose which in turn is changed to methyl cellulose by reaction with methylchloride gas. The finished granules are readily soluble. They are mixed with water 1 to 50 parts. Cellulose glue can be mixed with other binders and emulsified with oils. It is often used for wallpapering and bill-sticking and is excellent for pasting down large sheets of drawing paper on card or wood.

4. *Various gums, of which the best known is gum arabic*, are obtainable. Gum arabic is a resinous secretion from the acacia plant, and is sold in lumps. It is readily soluble in water, and remains so after drying; it is not weatherproof. It can be mixed with other binders and emulsified with oils and resins. Gum is used chiefly as a binder for tempera and water colours and pastel shades.

Synthetic resins

Synthetic resins are increasingly taking the place of natural glues by virtue of their better adhesive properties. There are two main types of resin adhesive. The first use thinners or hardeners to obtain a clean hard bond. They can be mixed to suit the work. The second type consists of the emulsion or dispersion resin thinned with water. The water solvent or dispersion agent evaporates or soaks into the materials during glueing. Materials are much less likely to distort when using these glues than with natural glues. Dispersion resins are used instead of casein glues in bookbinding, and also as bases for pigments, giving waterproof paints (emulsion paints).

Rubber solutions

The previously described adhesives all have a water base. This means that when glueing porous surfaces such as paper or card, there is bound to be a certain amount of distortion. This is not always tolerable, especially for accurate work with coloured sheets, or for pasting up plastic foil or photographs. With this in mind, waterless glues were developed which do not distort the materials and remain elastic. These glues consist of a solution of rubber in a volatile solvent. They work on the principle of contact adhesion. The two surfaces to be joined are coated thinly with the solution and allowed to dry. On coming into contact under light pressure they stick firmly. If you make a mistake in positioning you can generally pull the two apart again. If they have been stuck for a long time, dissolve the adhesive with benzine.

Artists' colours

The colours used by artists consist of pigment mixed in powder form with a liquid binder to produce a coloured solution or paste. Insoluble pigments are generally used; they are held in suspension in the fluid medium. Soluble dyes are less used. Some of them produce very bright colours, but generally they do not have such good light-fastness as pigments.

Tempera colours

Tempera colours consist of an emulsion of pigment and a fluid medium. There are two kinds, casein tempera colours and gum tempera colours. You can mix your own colours. Make sure the medium has the right consistency. It should dissolve in water, but pigment and medium should not separate on application to the paper.

1. *Casein tempera*. Stir 1 part of insoluble pure casein into 5 parts of water and warm until the casein has swelled. To dissolve the casein mix a solution of 0·3 parts of borax, potash, or carbonate of ammonia in a little water, and stir it into the casein container. Carbon dioxide is given off during boiling, and the solution is ready after stirring. Ammonia casein keeps well in bottles. To mix the colours for use, make a paste of the pigment with a little water and stir into casein solution. Add three parts of water to obtain a brushing consistency.

   Casein tempera is insoluble in water (washable) and

can be mixed with oils if required. Take 1 part of boiled linseed oil and 4 parts of casein size. Pour them into a bottle (first oil, then water) and shake them well together.

2. *Gum tempera.* The proprietary brands of tempera colours usually use a gum base. This medium stores well and the colours do not spoil. To make your own colours, mix 1 part powdered gum arabic with 3 parts water and 5 per cent glycerine as a softener. Mix the thick solution with an oil medium. Boiled linseed oil gives a rich, oily emulsion, and dammar varnish a thinner one. Combine 5 parts of gum solution with 1 part of oil. The colour is not washable.

Water colours

Water colours consist of very finely ground earth, mineral, and aniline colours with a dextrin or gum arabic medium mixed with glycerine to keep the colour blocks soft. The colours are bought ready made. The colours are mechanically ground, and thickened under heat. The paste is rolled into sheets and stamped into little round or square blocks. These are pressed into small porcelain or earthenware containers. Water colours can also be bought in paste form in tubes. Water colours are transparent and can be worked evenly on a slightly damp surface. Water colour paper is best, but any white, suitably sized paper will do. The fastness varies from colour to colour.

Silk-screen colours

Especially finely ground pigments are used for silk-screen printing colours. Dye colours are used for transparent printing. The colours must have a jelly consistency and yet flow under pressure from the squeegee. The colours dry relatively quickly: matt colours take about 15–30 minutes and glossy colours a little longer.

Drawing ink

Ink can be bought in solid form, to be ground and diluted, or in liquid form. It is generally known as indian ink.

1. *Black ink sticks.* The basis of solid indian ink is carbon black from various oils and woods. Skin glue is used as a medium, and carbolic acid and camphor are added to combat mildewing. The constituents are mechanically ground together into a paste. This is formed into

sticks and dried. Before use grind the ink together with water in a porcelain dish. The longer you stir, the darker will be the ink as more dissolves.

2. *Liquid indian ink.* The medium for liquid indian ink is a weak shellac solution. The shellac is brought into solution with the help of borax. This is mixed mechanically with the lamp black to give a fine suspension. The particles are so fine that they do not clump or sink to form a sediment. The ink dries semi-matt or glossy and is waterproof. Water-based indian inks are also available.

3. *Coloured inks.* Coloured inks consist of dyes dissolved in a weak shellac solution. They are waterproof when dry, but the colours are not very fast. They can be diluted a little but only with distilled water.

4. *Coloured pigment inks.* Shellac is again the medium, but the colour takes the form of a suspended pigment. The pigment tends to settle and the ink must be shaken well before use. The ink can be thinned a little with distilled water.

5. *Ink in tubes.* Ink can be bought in tubes in a paste form. It has a shellac medium and can be mixed with liquid inks but not with tempera colours. It dries matt.

Dye colours

Dye colours are made from selected dyes having relatively good light-fastness, with a little binder, usually gum arabic or gelatine. They are used mainly for colouring or tinting matt or glossy photographs. They are transparent when thinned with water and can be mixed with one another. Dyes penetrate a porous surface, colouring it permanently.

Coloured crayons

Crayons are composed of pigment, filler and various binders. They are supplied as pastels, wax crayons, or copying crayons.

Pastels consist of fast pigments and filler, usually clay (kaolin) or gypsum, held together by cellulose size. The finished pastels are often wrapped with paper. Pastel drawings tend to smear and must be treated with fixative (see page 201).

Wax crayons use wax or various fats to bind the pigment and fillers together. They cannot be dissolved in water.

Copying crayons contain the usual pigments, filler and binder, but have a lubricant added in the form of

water-soluble fats or soaps. In the manufacturing process, the coloured paste is squeezed through different sized nozzles and then dried in sticks. The thinner sticks are encased in wood to make coloured pencils, and the thicker ones wrapped in paper. Copying crayon can be completely dissolved to form a wash with water. Semi-waterproof crayons are partly soluble in water, but the marks made with them on paper are water resistant.

Fixatives

Chalk, charcoal, and pastel drawings are made permanent with fixatives. These are liquids which are sprayed on to the drawing to hold down the individual pigment grains. Fixatives are dilute solutions of one of the following resins: mastic, dammar rosin, or shellac. Suitable solvents are: alcohol, petrol, benzine, or ether.

The following are recipes for home-made fixatives:
1. 2 parts of bleached shellac
98 parts alcohol
2. 2 parts venetian turpentine
98 parts alcohol
3. Dissolve 2 parts of mastic in ether and make up to 100 parts with alcohol
4. 2 parts dammar resin
98 parts pure petrol
5. 2 parts resin
98 parts petrol, ether, or alcohol

Fixatives should be colourless and dry matt and quickly. They should not discolour the colour or paper, even with time. For this reason, shellac, dammar, and mastic are preferred to resin.

Primers

For painting on card, hardboard, wood, linen, or brown paper, it is necessary to prime the surface first. These surfaces are not suitable in their natural state: the colour becomes dead, or does not take properly, and transparent colours are completely lost. The final effect of the design depends to a great extent on the quality of the priming coat. Primers contain filler, a body colour, and a medium. Precipitated chalk, gypsum (light spar), kaolin, pearl white, or marble dust are suitable as fillers. Zinc white or lithopone (fast) can be used as body colours. The binder can be skin glue, casein glue, or dispersion glue.

1. *Chalk primer.* A suitable chalk primer consists of an undercoating of 3 oz. (80 gm.) of skin glue to 2 pints (1 litre) of water followed by a primer made from 1 part gypsum or precipitated chalk, 1 part zinc white, 1–3 parts water, and 1 part warm glue.

   Moisten the surface with a cloth (remove the impregnated surface of hardboard by sanding). Give one coat of size to seal the pores, and then when the surface is dry, apply the primer with a brush or knife. Mix the primer with 3 parts water for brushing, and with one part for a knife. Lay on 2–3 coats of primer, letting each coat dry in between. The final coat can be scraped or sanded to give a smooth surface. If necessary, brush on a final coat of size: consisting of 1 part casein glue with 3 parts water.

2. *Casein primer.* First make a binder from 2 oz. (50 gm.) casein powder to 1 pint ($\frac{1}{2}$ litre) water. Stir the powder into the water and warm to swell the casein. Add 230 grains (15 gm.) borax, potash, or carbonate of ammonia to disintegrate the casein. The mixture gives off carbon dioxide and then is ready for use.

   Undercoating and size are made from 1 part casein solution to 3 parts water.

   The primer itself consists of 1 part gypsum, 1 part zinc white, 2 parts water, and 1 part casein solution. Mix the ingredients to a thin paste. Wait until the undercoat is dry and then lay on 2–3 coats of primer, allowing half an hour in between. This casein primer is not as porous as the chalk primer, but you may sand it and give a coat of size if you wish.

3. *Emulsion primer.* The undercoat consists of 1 part synthetic resin emulsion to 2 parts water.

   The primer is prepared from 1 part precipitated chalk or light spar, 2 parts water and 1 part emulsion.

   The size is 1 part emulsion to 3–5 parts water.

   This primer is easy to make up and keeps well. It is good for both tempera and casein colours. You may sand the surface for a smoother finish.

4. *Watercolour primer.* It is essential for good designs that the colour of the paint remains true even when dry. To prepare poorer papers for water-colour painting coat the surface with a size consisting of 1 part cellulose size, gum arabic, or dextrin to 3–5 parts water.

   This size will also size chalk, casein, and emulsion primers ready for water-colour painting. In this case thin the size with 2–3 parts water.

5. *Primers for pastel.* To prepare paper, card, or board for

pastels, brush on a coat of starch size and dust the wet sheet with pumice-stone powder. Tap off the superfluous powder. The surface is ready for use when it is dry.

Glueing and mounting

Presentation is an important part of any design project. An untidy, dog-eared design is certain to make a worse impression than a cleanly-detailed, well presented job. To make a design more permanent and to protect it from rough handling it is as well to mount it on a stiff backing. Larger designs may even be cloth backed.

Using rubber cement

Rubber cement can be used to mount work on all thicknesses of backing without having to stick a compensating sheet on the back. Water-soluble glues tend to swell the paper. A quite thin paper glued with such a glue will shrink and warp even a thick board on drying. Rubber cement contains no water and all surfaces adhered with it will remain flat. The method of using rubber cement was described on page 198. A method for sticking thin foils is given on page 155. Rubber cement can be used for the following jobs:

1. Layouts (sticking type and illustrations)
2. Mounting photographs
3. Photomontage (cut and paste)
4. Coloured paper work (print and fabric designs, etc.)
5. Mounting delicate drawings
6. Presentation mounting

It is important not to roll sheets stuck with rubber

Using rubber cement. A sheet of tracing paper is laid between the two sheets

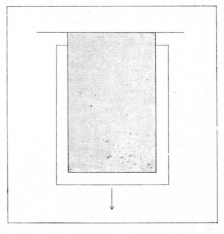

cement. The glue remains elastic, and the surface will part and crease.

Mounting

Experience and a good knowledge of the different properties of glue and paste are required to use water-based adhesives. Glue has a small water content and sticks strongly, whereas paste contains much water and does not stick so well. As paste contains so much water the paper stretches more than with glue. The tension obtained as the paper shrinks again is also much greater and the paper lies closer to the base. For this reason the base structure shows through much more than with glued sheets.

Smooth bases should therefore be used for paste mountings. When using water-based pastes it is advisable to stretch another sheet on the back of the mount. Always use paste where a good tension is needed.

These differences can be used to good advantage to even out tensions by a skilful use of paste and glue. It is important to watch the machine direction of the paper. The paper stretches and shrinks most across the machine direction, so you must always stick the backing sheet in the same direction. This equalizes the tension and the mount is absolutely flat on drying.

Pasting

Cut the sheet to be mounted roughly to size, leaving a bit extra all round. Lay it face down on the table corner so that two sides hang over about ½ in. (1 cm.). Now lay on the paste with a brush, working away from the

Pasting a sheet of paper. The sheet protrudes about ½ in. over the table edge on two sides.

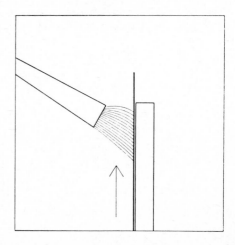

middle of the sheet. When this half is covered, turn the sheet through 180° and cover the other half. Use a large, soft brush. This will enable you to cover the surface quickly and evenly. The brush-strokes should always be at right-angles to the paper edge, never parallel to it, or you may get paste on to the face of the paper. Finally look over the surface against the light to check that it is completely covered. Dry bits will appear matt. Make certain that there are no lumps, dirt or brush bristles stuck in with the paste. There is nothing you can do about them later.

Lay paste on thicker than glue. Leave pasted sides to stretch for 2–3 minutes before sticking them. Stick glued sides immediately after coating.

Lift the sheet up by two opposite corners and lay one side along the mount, adjusting the position. When all is right, gently lay the sheet flat on the mount. Get someone to help you with larger sheets. Now lay a clean sheet of thin paper over the work. Starting at the middle and working outwards, press out all the air bubbles with the ball of your hand. Paper the back of the mount in the same way and then press it under a weighted board until it is dry. When the work is mounted on a thick wooden board, it can be laid horizontally on two chair backs and left to dry.

Mounting in practice

Here are a few examples of the actual mounting of finished work:

1. *Base:* card, hardboard, or chipboard
   Work: photographic paper
   Mounting: folded edges
   Adhesive: glue
   Backing: paper of similar thickness
   Backing adhesive: paste
   When the edges of the work are turned over the mount and stuck down, the mount will be warped much more during drying. It is better to paper the back with a paper of the same thickness as on the front. Cut the work roughly to size, leaving about $1\frac{1}{4}$ in. (3 cm.) spare all round. Stick the sheet down with an even margin. Now trim the edges to a width of $\frac{1}{2}$–$\frac{3}{4}$ in. (10–20 cm.) plus the thickness of the mount. Fold the edges over, opposite sides first, and mitre the corners as if you were packing a parcel. Press the edges down well with a clean cloth. Cut the backing paper a little smaller than

the mount. Leave it to stretch after pasting, and then stick it down as usual.

2. *Base:* card, hardboard, or chipboard
Work: photographic paper
Mounting: trimmed edges
Adhesive: glue
Backing: thin brown paper
Backing adhesive: paste
Here the edges are not folded over, so you must rub them down well. The glue tends to dry more quickly at the edges, and especially at the corners. The edges tend to peel away and the corners will stand up. To prevent this, weight the corners down with wooden blocks or other suitable weights. Trim the edges with a razor or sharp knife when the glue is dry.

3. *Base:* hardboard or chipboard
Work: wet photographic paper
Mounting: trimmed edges
Adhesive: glue
Backing: paper of similar thickness
Backing adhesive: glue
You can mount photographs straight from the rinsing bath. Let the surplus water drip away and lay the print face down on a sheet of glass. Apply the glue to the back. Soak a paper of similar thickness as a backing sheet and glue it in the same way.

4. *Base:* card, hardboard, or chipboard
Work: glossy photograph
Mounting: trimmed edges
Adhesive: glue
Backing: thin paper
Backing adhesive: paste
Absolute cleanliness is essential when mounting glossy prints. One spot of glue on the print surface will ruin the work. It is better to mount the backing sheet first, and to leave the photo itself until last.

A safer method is to use dry-mounting tissue (see page 207).

5. *Base:* card, hardboard, or chipboard
Work: drawing paper or card
Mounting: trimmed edges
Adhesive: $\frac{1}{2}$ glue, $\frac{1}{2}$ paste
Backing: thin paper, drawing paper or card of similar thickness
Backing adhesive: paste or $\frac{1}{2}$ glue, $\frac{1}{2}$ paste
Take great care in mounting work done in water-colours. It is better to mount the paper first and then

to do the design later. A mixture of one part of cellulose or starch paste to one part of synthetic resin glue sticks well. Thick drawing cards must be firmly stuck to the base board to prevent blisters forming when the card is wet by the colour. The paste and glue mixture not only sticks well, but ensures that the paper is well stretched. This also hinders the formation of bubbles.

6. *Base:* card, hardboard, or chipboard
   Work: printed posters, or thin paper
   Mounting: trimmed edges
   Adhesive: paste
   Backing: paper of similar thickness
   Backing adhesive: paste
   Use less glue in the mixture for thicker papers.

7. *Base:* canvas
   Work: trimmed edges
   Adhesive: paste
   The great advantage of mounting work on canvas is that it can be rolled up. It needs no backing sheet. Cut the canvas about 4 in. (10 cm.) longer and wider than the work. Next, the canvas must be stretched on a large board. Glue a strip along the edges of the sheet about 1 in. (2·5 cm.) wide. Mask this strip off using a piece of paper. This will make it easier to spread the glue evenly. Lay the glued canvas on the board and spread it out flat. Press the edges down well so that they stick firmly to the wood. When the glue is dry, damp the canvas with a wet sponge so that as it dries again it shrinks and tensions itself. Paste the back of the work to be mounted and press it well down on the canvas. Leave the job to dry well and then cut it out with a sharp knife and metal straightedge.

Dry-mounting photographs

Glossy prints can be mounted quickly and cleanly on almost any base with mounting tissue. Cut the tissue a little larger than the print. Stick it down to the back of the print by touching it with the point of a warm iron in several spots. This melts the resin in the tissue and makes it stick. Now trim the print and tissue to the finished size, and position it on the mount. Lay a protecting sheet of card over the face and press it down with a hot iron. There is no need for a backing sheet on this kind of mount.

Binding

The task of binding completes the stages of design and planning, and the bound pages of a magazine, a catalogue, or a book, represent the finished printed work. It is by no means unimportant which form of binding is used. The binding should be thought of as an integrated part of the design and production, and it should be borne in mind when fixing the price. The method of folding plays an important part and should also be planned with the design. The following section deals with the different methods of folding and binding

Folding methods

The unfolded sheets, or broadsides, can be folded in several ways; there is right-angle folding, parallel folding, and many miscellaneous foldings. Folding machines, working semi- or fully automatically, can handle 3,500–5,000 sheets an hour, depending on the method of folding.

1. *Right-angle folding*. This type is mainly used for books and newspapers. The paper is folded two, three, or four times.
2. *Parallel folding*. Parallel folding offers an exceptionally large range of possibilities. It is used chiefly for leaflets and so on. All the folds run parallel either in concertina fashion or in the form of a flat roll.
3. *Mixed folding*. This is a combination of right-angle and parallel folding.
4. *Folding in quires*. Here several sheets of paper are folded together. This method is used for notebooks and exercise books.

Right-angle folding

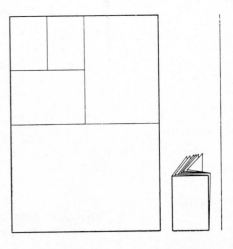

Varieties of fold:
1 Parallel
2 Concertina
3, 4 Miscellaneous
5 Folding in quires
6 Gathered sheets
7 Inset sheets

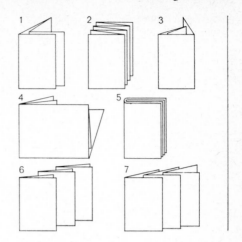

Binding methods

There are two ways of assembling the folded sheets. They may be "gathered" or "inset". In the first case the folded sheets are stacked one on top of the other, and in the second case are inserted into one another. The sheets are stitched together with thread or wire. Gathered sheets are sewn together on a book sewing machine. Inset sheets are joined with wire staples on a wire stitcher or stapler.

Thread sewing takes various forms:

1. *Pamphlet stitching*. Exercise books are stitched with two or three stitches. The ends of the thread are knotted.
2. *French sewn*. This method is simple and cheap. The sheets are held together with thread and glue.
3. *Sewing through linen*. Books are usually bound in this way. The linen ensures a firm hold, especially when a large number of sheets must be bound together.
4. *Sewing on hemp cords*. The sheets are sewn over cords. These are flattened so that they do not show through the spine.
5. *Sewing on tapes*. Account books, note books, etc., are often sewn this way. Valuable parchment pages are often sewn on strips of leather or parchment.
6. *Sawn-in sewing*. Nicks are sawn into the sheets so that the cords do not protrude on the spine. On the other hand the pages are defaced.
7. *Sewing on raised cords*. Here the cords are deliberately left standing to show through the spine. This method is antiquated.

Materials

Stitching methods:
1 Knotted stitching

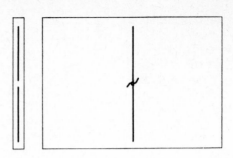

2 Oversewn with thread

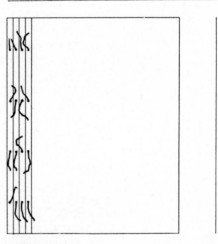

3 Sewn through linen

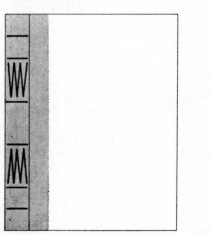

4 Sewn on hemp cords

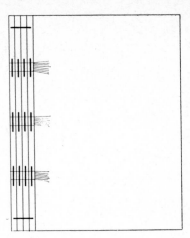

5 Sewn on tapes

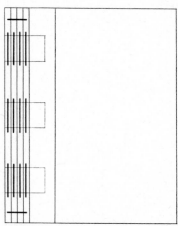

6 Sawn-in sewing

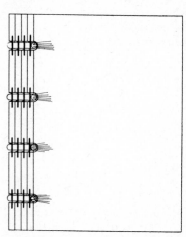

Materials

7 Saddle stitching (with wire staples)

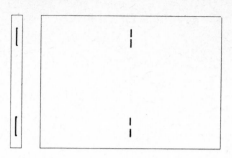

8 Side stitching or stabbing

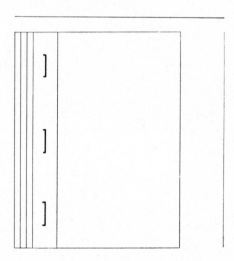

Fan binding:
1 Glueing the edges of pages
2 Pressing the block of paper

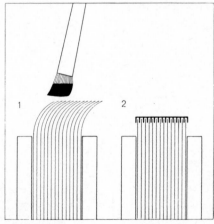

Wire stitching, or stapling, is widely used for exercise books, notepads, catalogues, and magazines. It takes two forms:

1. *Saddle stitching*. This process is used for inset pages in magazines, etc. The pages are stapled in the fold. The ends of the staple are always inside.
2. *Side stitching, stabbing*. Note blocks, etc., are often side stitched. The disadvantages of this method are that the pages are difficult to open and read and that the pages themselves are slightly defaced by the stitching.
3. *Perfect or unsewn binding*. Another process for binding single sheets is by "perfect" or unsewn binding. The sheets are cut straight and then bent to one side. This exposes a small area of each sheet, which is then glued. The sheets are then bent and glued on the other side, and put in a press. A sheet of linen is pressed into the glue on the spine.

Binding materials
Booklets

The different bindings are named after the uses to which they are put. Booklets are divided into two types—paperbacked and quarter cloth bound.

1. *Paperback binding*. The pages are french sewn or stapled, trimmed, glued in a block, and stuck into the cover. The cover is made of stiff card and is usually scored four times. In the simplest bindings, the cover is stuck only along the back. This is the cheapest type of binding. Scoring is done in two ways. In one the fibres of the card are loosened along the fold line, but the card is not weakened. In the other, a cut is made in

Binding methods:
1 Paperback

the card, weakening it here. This method is used mainly for packages.

2.   *Quarter cloth binding.* Quarter cloth booklets are sewn on cords or tapes and have separate card covers and sometimes a linen back. An end paper is stuck between the cover and first page.

Cloth and board binding

As well as linen, calico and synthetic materials are used for cloth bindings. The main feature of these bindings is their durability, unlike the booklets. The pages are sewn on tapes or through linen. The cover is of stiff card and is covered with cloth together with the back. The finished book block is sometimes pressed to give a cover with a rounded back.

2 Quarter cloth

3 Cloth

1. *Quarter cloth binding.* Quarter cloth binding is cheaper than cloth binding. Only the back is covered in cloth; the covers are clad only in paper.
2. *Cloth binding.* Cloth binding is easier to do than quarter cloth binding as the whole cover can be made together in one piece.
3. *Board binding.* The only difference between this and cloth binding is that the covering is of paper instead of linen.
4. *Plastic binding.* The covers and back of the book are covered on both sides with PVC foil (polyvinylchloride) welded at the edges. The pages are sewn through linen and glued into the finished covers. End-papers are glued in with special adhesive. Sometimes the covers are made solely out of plastic, without a board stiffening. Plastic foil can be obtained with a smooth surface or with a large variety of textures. Lettering can be silk-screened on to the plastic with special colours. Recently, special materials treated on the surface with a plastic solution (PVC) have become available. This material can be embossed. The advantages of plastic covers are that they are tough, washable, do not show scrubs and scratches, and are not affected by fats and oils.

Full- and half-binding, vellum bindings

The leather binding process is similar to cloth binding. Usually the two are combined: the back is covered in leather, and the case in cloth. Gold leaf can be used on leather. Quarter vellum and full vellum bindings are used for de luxe editions. Vellum is very tough and can distort the covers. Earlier, bookbinders used wood instead of board for vellum covers. Today, aluminium is often used. The backs of half- and full-bindings are given special treatment with the cords showing through. The back and corners of a half-bound book are covered in a different material from the covers, usually leather, and some books are still bound fully in leather.

Special bindings

Spiral or plastic bindings are widely used for catalogues, calenders, sample booklets, and so on. Each sheet is stamped with a row of holes through which the wire or plastic is threaded to hold the pages together. One great advantage of this binding is that the

4 Spiral

open sheets lie absolutely flat. There are also plastic ring bindings which allow the pages to be removed and replaced.

Embossing

The title, vignette, or other device is embossed on the finished case in an embossing press. The tool is a stereo taken from a block or a type forme (see page 41). The quality of the embossing depends on the surface of the material. Embossing is easiest on smooth materials, but with coarse linen a blank impression must be made first without any ink or foil (blind blocking) and a second impression with ink or foil. Foils are better suited for white or light-coloured impressions. These foils are of various types. They consist of a base foil with a thin layer of colour. A hot tool is used for embossing, and the colour layer separates from the foil and remains on the case. Similar foils are used for gold and silver embossing.

When designing an embossed cover, avoid designs with very fine lines, or lettering with thin hair lines or serifs. Do not let the design go too near the edges of the cover. The cover is more flexible at the edges and this leads to uneven embossing. Also the linen covering is turned over the edge of the case and the double thickness here leads to heavier embossing.

LIGHTING FOR PHOTOGRAPHY

Good photography is as much dependent on effective lighting as it is on good picture composition.

Daylight

The sun is nature's main light source. Its varying positions in relation to the subject enable it to provide the following basic types of lighting:

Direct frontal lighting—with the sun more or less directly behind the camera position,

Oblique lighting—with the sun behind, but distinctly to one side of the camera position,

Back-lighting—with the sun behind the subject.

The kind of lighting used affects the nature of picture obtained. Oblique or side-lighting gives good modelling, with distinct shadows, and can be regarded as a useful "general purpose" type. Direct lighting is inclined to produce flat, low-contrast results. Back-lighting tends to yield a silhouette image, and if good detail is required in the subject matter, this type of lighting calls for a considerable increase in exposure. To assure an acceptable rendering of both highlight areas and shadow detail, when both lighting and subject matter are fairly contrasty, the exposure given should be a mean between the exposure meter readings indicated for the deepest shadow and the brightest highlight that are to be reproduced with detail. When shooting against the light it is advisable to use an efficient lens hood.

Both the time of day and weather conditions affect the nature of outdoor lighting. When photographing buildings, outdoor sculpture, bridges and the like, it is important to determine, and wait for, the right conditions. A completely overcast sky gives a soft and shadowless light while a cloudless sunny sky leads to deep shadows. A sunny sky with some cloud also gives a fairly contrasty lighting, although the clouds act as reflectors, lightening the shadows somewhat.

Artificial lights in the studio can be moved into any required position, but outdoors it is a case of waiting for the right position of the sun, and the desired weather conditions. It is worthwhile remembering that the eerie lighting which precedes a storm or the fairy-tale atmosphere of an early morning mist often lead to far more satisfying landscape pictures than do the conditions on a fine sunny day.

The best general condition for architectural photography is direct sunlight, with some cloud in the sky. This gives good contrast, and at the same time assures some shadow detail. Ideally, the most important side of the building should be in direct sunlight, and the side at right-angles to it in moderate shadow.

A yellow, orange or red filter can be used to increase the contrast between a white concrete building and the blue sky to a greater or lesser extent.

Artificial light

The general artificial light sources for photography are the flash bulb, the electronic flash unit and the tungsten-filament lamp. Flash provides a high intensity of illumination for a short time, enabling fast action to be stopped. The continuously burning tungsten lamp, on the other hand, has the advantage of giving the photographer complete visual control of his lighting effects.

The standard general-purpose filament lamp for studio photography is the photoflood. There are a number of types, varying in light output. These floods should be used in specially designed reflectors.

If the subject matter is such as to permit comparatively long exposures, then it is quite possible to use ordinary household lamps, so long as only black-and-white film is being used.

Panchromatic film is sensitive to red, and orthochromatic is not. As tungsten lighting contains a high proportion of red, the former type of film should be used. If colour film is used, it must be of the type designed to be used in artificial light.

The intensity of the illumination reaching an object from a lamp varies in inverse proportion to the lamp–object distance. In other words, an object 1 yd. from a lamp is lit four times more intensely than it would be if it were 2 yds. from the same lamp.

Arranging the lamps

The basic types of lighting possible with one lamp can be compared with those possible with the sun, which

Lighting arrangements:
1 Direct or frontal

2 Bright side

3 Overhead

4 Back

5 **One** lamp and reflecting screen

6 Two lamps

have already been described. A direct frontal light gives an efficient but flat illumination. The shadows fall behind the subject, and can sometimes be completely hidden by it. A frontal light distinctly to one side of the camera lends some modelling to the subject, but also causes deep shadows. An overhead light, directly above the subject, gives an even illumination of the top of the subject, but is not satisfactory for most purposes. Shadows on the base are minimized in size, but shadows on the person or object being photographed tend to be excessive, and unnatural. Back-lighting renders the subject in silhouette, but gives it an outline or "rim-lighting".

The single lamp can be an effective tool to achieve special effects, but for most photography more than one lamp is called for. The simplest lighting system is the single lamp and the reflector screen. This screen can consist simply of white paper or card, of aluminium foil, of a specially designed umbrella, or of one of numerous other possible designs. The main function of the screen is to catch some of the light from the lamp, and reflect it back to lighten the shadows which this lamp has cast.

Two lamps can serve basically the same purpose as one lamp and a reflector. The main light is placed in front of, and slightly to one side of the subject. The second light is placed in front of and slightly to the other side, but at a greater distance from the subject, or it can be less powerful. The first light forms the main illumination, providing the modelling, and the second is the fill-in light, providing detail in the shadows.

If a reflector is used as fill-in, the second lamp can be used to achieve some special effect. It can, for example, be placed behind and to the side of the subject, to provide it with rim-lighting, or to give a highlight to the hair of a sitter.

Lighting silver and glass

The light tent is a useful tool in the photography of highly reflective objects, such as silverware. It eliminates both bright reflections from lamps and also dark areas caused by the reflection of dark objects around the studio. Thus silver can be photographed to really look like silver.

The light tent is easily constructed. Build a skeleton pyramid (a cube or cylinder will do, too) of wood or

A pyramidal light tent

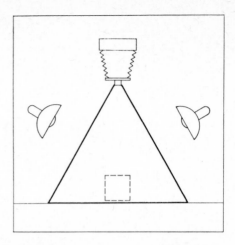

wire, and cover all sides with translucent white paper or cloth. Cut a small hole in one side, just large enough to take the camera lens. Lay the object to be photographed on a sheet of white paper, place the tent over it, and poke the camera lens through its hole. It now only remains to illuminate the tent evenly from the outside, and photography can begin.

Glass objects and rounded metal articles are particularly difficult to photograph, because each light source tends to produce its own highlights and reflections. The light tent could again be the answer but, unfortunately, it generally produces flat and uninteresting results. A more satisfactory solution is the moving lamp, or "painting with light".

The subject is first lit normally with one or two diffused lamps from the side and slightly behind it, these being carefully positioned so that there are no unwanted highlights. A third lamp is used to place highlights just exactly where they are wanted. To prevent unpleasant "spot" highlights, this lamp is moved back and forth during exposure, literally painting in highlight areas where they are wanted. The camera lens should be stopped well down, to give an exposure time which is comfortably long.

Avoiding highlights

Even with diffused lighting it is not always possible to avoid all reflections on shiny objects. There are other solutions. One of a number of methods can be used to render the shiny surfaces matt; alternatively, some reflections can be filtered out.

Glass photographed without highlights

A polished surface can be made dull by allowing the magnesium oxide given off by a burning magnesium strip to be deposited upon it. Metal containers can be filled with ice-cold water, which causes light condensation to form on their outer surface, thus dulling them. Spray bottles containing a special dulling liquid are available commercially.

Reflections of light from most non-metallic objects can be reduced or, in some cases, eliminated altogether by the use of a polarising filter. The degree of reduction possible depends on the angle at which the incident light hits the surface.

Silhouettes

Silhouettes can be photographed in two basic ways. The first uses a brightly illuminated white wall or

A silhouette effect. The cherries, not being transparent, give completely black silhouettes

screen in a large room kept as dark as possible. The best light in such a case is the spotlight, which minimizes the scatter of light. The subject is placed between the camera and the wall, and as far away from the wall as possible, great care being taken to ensure that no light reaches the side of the subject that is to be photographed.

Alternatively, a translucent white screen can be placed between the subject and the camera, the shadow of the subject being projected on to the screen by means of a focused spotlight. Care must be taken to see that the naked spotlight is not seen at the camera position through the screen.

High key and low key

A high-key picture is almost entirely at the light end of the tonal scale, there being only tiny areas of darker tone, such as the pupils of the eyes, nostrils, and the like. High-key photography calls for even frontal lighting, and a well-lit background of light colour. An ideal arrangement would consist of two banks of diffused lighting, symmetrically placed, one to each side of the subject, and one individual flood, placed to one side and at such a distance as to cast the very faintest of shadows. The flood helps to put a degree of modelling into the picture.

High-key lighting is more suitable to the photography of women and children, rather than men and, furthermore, it is only suited to those subjects who have a light skin, fair hair, and light eyes.

Low-key lighting has an effect opposite to that

High-key effect

Low-key effect

created by the high-key technique. It is inclined to suggest heaviness, sombreness and strength, and is most suitable for the dramatic portrayal of men. Low-key lighting is based on deep and extensive shadow areas. The lighting should be rather contrasty, and exposures should be calculated carefully, to ensure some detail in the shadows, while at the same time preventing burnt-out highlights.

BACKGROUNDS FOR PHOTOGRAPHY

The choice of background must be dependent on the subject matter, the type of lighting to be used, and on the effect that is aimed for but, generally speaking, a dark object will stand out better from a light background, and a light object from a dark background. Most straight advertising or catalogue photography calls for an article to be shot against an even-toned background.

A curved backing paper structure for photographs with a white background

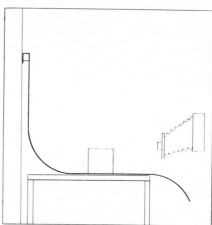

A white-background photograph

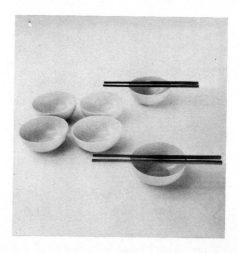

The shadows cannot be eliminated when the subject lies directly on the white background

The shadows can be eliminated by laying the subject on a sheet of glass above the background

The transition from floor to wall must be in the form of a continuous curve, so that there is no hard line across the picture area. A large sheet of paper, draped down the wall and then smoothly along the floor or over a table, is the ideal solution. All but black backgrounds should be illuminated evenly over the entire picture area unless, of course, special effects, such as spots or projected shapes, are aimed for.

Entirely shadowless lighting is sometimes desirable, but is difficult to achieve on a normal paper background. The solution lies in the separation of the subject matter from its shadow by laying it on a clean sheet of plate glass some one to two feet above a horizontally positioned sheet of white paper. The sheet of paper is evenly illuminated, and the subject matter can then be

229

A geometrically-arranged composition
on a black background

lit in such a way that the shadow cast on the background does not touch the subject at any point and can therefore lie beyond the bounds of the picture area. The camera is, of course, pointing down on this arrangement.

An alternative method would be to photograph the subject matter lying on a raised sheet of ground glass. In this case the shadows cast upon the top surface of the glass by the subject can be eliminated by illuminating the glass from below to the required extent.

Black backgrounds must be of a matt surface so that reflections from them can be kept to a minimum. The velvet type of surface, which absorbs most of the light that strikes it, is ideal. For small objects, a very efficient black background can be easily constructed by painting the inside surfaces of a large open box a matt black, or lining it with matt black paper.

Isolating picture elements

The aim in advertising photography is frequently the isolation, or emphasis, of important picture elements. Those parts of the picture which are to catch the viewer's immediate attention, must be made to stand out in some way. The background only establishes the scene and the atmosphere, and must be subdued. Sometimes it must be eliminated altogether.

The simplest way of isolating the subject is, of course, to photograph it before a background of uniform tone. But this is not usually a pictorially satisfactory solution.

By carefully limiting the depth of field within the scene, it is possible to retain the important part of the subject matter in sharp focus, while throwing the remainder out of focus. This selective focusing is most effective in emphasizing specific picture elements. It should be remembered that, at a given shooting distance, the longer the focal length of the camera lens, and the wider the lens aperture, the more limited will be the depth of field.

A contrast in the surface or texture of the subject and its background can do much to make the subject stand out. A highly polished object would appear prominent on a matt type of base, for example.

The lighting technique employed can be designed to lend prominence to some particular feature or item in a picture.

Movement of subject or camera during exposure

An impression of depth obtained through
differential focusing

causes blur on the resultant film, provided the exposure time is sufficiently long. This can be exploited for the purpose of emphasizing an element of the picture. If a fast-moving car is photographed with a stationary camera, the picture will show a blur of the car in sharp and "static" surroundings, but if the camera is swung to keep up with the car, the picture will reveal a sharply outlined car in blurred surroundings. This example not only "lifts out" the car from its background, but also serves the purpose of depicting the sensation of speed in a most convincing way.

It often occurs that a subject has to be photographed in a setting where the background is unavoidably untidy and distracting but where, nonetheless, a clean plain background is required in the finished picture.

The fixed camera renders the background sharp, but at slower shutter speeds moving objects are blurred.

Moving the camera to follow the car's movement renders the car sharply but blurs the background

This can be achieved by painting out, or blocking out, the background area on the negative—but this is only practicable if the negative is large enough, and if the outline of the main subject is not too complicated. To obtain a white background it is simply necessary to paint it out in the negative, and then print this. If a black background is required, a positive transparency must first be made of the negative. The background is then painted out on this, after which a negative is made once again. This final negative will have a clear background, which will print as black.

A black background on the print can also be attained by clearing the negative background with Farmer's reducer. This is best done by first carefully painting a protective mask of a special preparation on top of the image part that is to remain, applying the Farmer's reducer, washing and drying the film, and then removing the mask again in the manner indicated in the instruction material for the masking solution.

A subject can also be given uniform surroundings, either white or black, by painting out a disturbing background directly on the enlargement. Again, the contours of the main subject must be carefully outlined with a fine brush first, the remainder of the background surface being painted out as evenly as possible after that. For a print which is intended for block-making, careful brush work is usually good enough, but if the photographic print is to be the end-product, then a smoother and more satisfactory background surface can be achieved through the use of an air-brush. Before air-brushing the print, the important subject matter must first be masked carefully. With the aid of the air-brush it is possible to get not only good black or white backgrounds, but also very uniform shades of grey (see page 273).

A subject which has simple outlines, mostly of straight lines, can be cut out from an enlargement and stuck on to a sheet of card of the desired shade of grey. If necessary, this montage can then be re-photographed to yield a negative for quantity reproduction.

CAMERA TECHNIQUES

Perspective

A photograph has "correct" perspective only when it is viewed from the correct position. The correct viewing position is such that the angle subtended at the eye by the image field is the same as the angle that was subtended at the camera lens by the corresponding subject field. This means that for a correct perspective presentation a print must be viewed from a distance which is equal to the focal length of the camera lens used multiplied by the linear enlargement of the negative image. When a print is viewed from an appreciably greater distance, the depth of the picture will appear to be exaggerated, and when a print is viewed from too close up, the depth will appear foreshortened.

As the viewing distance for a print is usually fairly standard for one specific print size (regardless of what focal length lens was used to make the negative), it follows that long focal length lenses tend to produce prints in which the depth perspective is foreshortened, while wide-angle lenses tend to give us prints with excessive depth perspective. It should always be remembered that apparent distortion of perspective in the photograph is due entirely to "incorrect" viewing distance, and not merely to the focal length of the lens used.

Let us assume that a receding building is photographed on 4×5 in. film with a 5-in. lens, and also with a 10-in. lens from the same position. Each of the negatives is made into a 20×16-in. enlargement. The correct viewing distance for the first would be 20 in., and for the second it would be 40 in. The normal viewer is more likely to look at a 20×16-in. enlargement from 40 in. than 20 in., and as a result the "wide-angle" shot has the familiar perspective distortion. This, incidentally, is the reason why the familiar boat-race eight appear to be cramped into a far shorter boat to those viewers who are watching the movie newsreel from the front rows, than to those in the rear seats.

Another form of perspective distortion takes the form of the converging verticals in the tall building photographed with the camera tilted upwards. While the eye accepts this convergence of lines when looking at the real thing, it considers it wrong in the photograph.

For the vertical lines of a building to be reproduced parallel on the negative it is either necessary to point the camera absolutely horizontally during shooting, or to use a camera with movements, enabling the film plane to be kept vertical, i.e. parallel to the building face, even while the camera is being tilted upwards.

Vertical lines which converge in the negative can still be corrected at the enlarging stage. This is achieved by tilting the baseboard in such a way as to render the

Converging verticals in the negative can be corrected by tilting the paper during enlarging

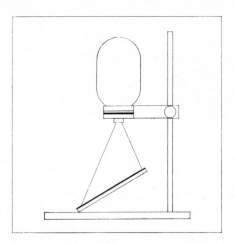

converging lines parallel. By also tilting the lens panel in the same direction, or the negative carrier in the opposite direction, to the desired degree, it is possible to regain overall sharpness of the image without the need for excessive stopping down of the lens.

Filters

Some of the "distortions" that a camera can produce are useful to achieve quite specific results. Perhaps the simplest tool for the distortion of reality is the coloured filter.

Coloured filters affect the grey tone scale on the negative. Through the use of filters, picture areas can be emphasized or subdued, and contrasts can be heightened or lessened. The classic example is the use

236

Correcting converging verticals:
1 When the camera is tilted, verticals converge
2 The verticals remain parallel when the camera is adjusted

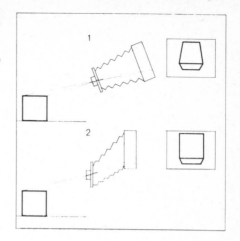

A picture taken with a tilted camera, showing converging verticals

When the camera is held level and the movements used, verticals remain parallel

Filters can be used to darken the tone of a
blue sky. A deep red filter can give a
quite dramatic effect

of the yellow, orange or red filter to increase the
contrast between white clouds and the blue sky.

If adjoining areas of blue and red reproduce as one
uniform shade of grey in the picture, this can be
remedied by using either a filter toward the red end of
the spectrum or one toward the blue end. This will
increase the contrast between the two shades. The
extreme is reached if a deep blue or deep red filter is
used, in which case the result will be nearly black and
white in the negative.

It should be remembered that a filter transmits its
own colour and absorbs the complementary colours.
Thus, a red filter will lighten red in the finished print,
and darken blue and green. All coloured filters have a
specific "filter factor", by which the normal exposure
must be increased with their use.

"Ghost" photography

Is it possible to show the inside of a machine which is
covered with an opaque housing? Yes, it is—through
the technique of double- or multiple-exposure. But it
can only be done with a completely black background.

To render the machine "transparent", our exposure
time must be split into two distinct parts. The first
exposure is given to the machine without its housing
and the second to the machine with the housing in
place, great care being taken that neither machine nor
camera are moved in the slightest degree between
exposures. Depending on the proportion in which the
total exposure time is split, it is possible to achieve a
greater or lesser degree of "transparency". If the

Phantom photography by double
exposure. One exposure was made with
the cover off and the carriage in the central
position. A shorter exposure was then made
with the cover replaced, the carriage
moved along and paper inserted

internal mechanism is the all-important feature, for example, this should be given about two-thirds of the exposure, the remaining third being given to the covered machine. By this method it is also possible to show various stages of an operation in one picture.

If a ghost picture of this type is required against a white background, it is necessary to make two or more separate negatives—each shot against a white background—and these must then be enlarged on one sheet of paper.

"Doubles"

Doubles pictures are made using a mask, and giving two exposures. A box, bellows or stiff cardboard tube is fixed over the lens panel, this fixture being of such a

A tube with two half-masks can be fitted to the camera to provide "double" or split-screen photographs

size that its outline falls just outside the film image area. A piece of black card covers exactly half of the opening of this box. The card should be in the region of 6 in. in front of the camera lens. Get your subject to occupy that side of the picture area which is not shielded, and give a normal correct exposure. Next mask the other half of the opening in the box, put the subject to the other side of the picture area, and give the same exposure again.

Care should be taken to assure that the masking is done accurately, without overlap or extra space in the middle, that the two exposure times are exactly equal, and that the camera does not move between exposures. The further the mask is from the camera lens, the sharper will be the division between the two picture halves. The shorter the box or bellows, the more "fuzzy" will be the border. Ideally, the division line should coincide with some natural vertical line in the picture such as a door-post, the corner of a room, or the like. In this way any visible outline will be concealed as much as possible. The double character can, of course, enact all kinds of activities with himself in the two picture halves, so long as he never extends beyond the middle line.

Stroboscopic-type pictures

The stroboscope makes it possible to record several stages or positions of a continuous movement on a single negative. In the moving film, a number of frames are required to record a movement. In "ghost" photography each stage in the movement must be newly posed, whereas the stroboscopic technique enables us to register natural and continuous movements, as they are actually happening. It can be used to show, for example, the movements made by a complex tool and by the operator using it. It can be used to produce a multiple picture of a golfer swinging a club, the sequence of distinct positions in the movement shown on the one print enabling the student to analyze the swing in detail.

The proper equipment for stroboscopic photography consists of an electronic flash apparatus which gives a fast and regularly-spaced sequence of short flashes. This lights the subject, which must be placed before a completely black background. The camera shutter must, of course, remain open for the duration of the flash sequence that is to be registered.

Apparatus for stroboscopic photography:
1 Sheet metal disc
2 Rectangular slit
3 Camera
4 Drive (electric motor)
5 Spindle
6 Extension tube

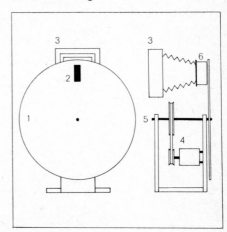

Such equipment is very expensive, and not generally available to the average photographer, but perfectly satisfactory results can be obtained with a quite simple form of stroboscope, which can be home-constructed. From a metal sheet about $\frac{1}{32}$ in. thick, cut a circular disc about 12 in. in diameter. About $\frac{3}{4}$ in. from the edge of the disc cut a rectangular hole, with the side facing in the radial direction slightly longer than the diameter of the front of the camera lens and the side in the tangential direction about half that length.

Mount the disc firmly on an axle which turns, if possible, on ball bearings. (The hub of an old bicycle will do the job.) Fix the whole assembly on a stand which allows the disc to turn freely in a vertical plane. A method of driving the disc must now be found, and this is best achieved through a small electric motor, in conjunction with some kind of belt drive. Paint the disc matt black, to eliminate the danger of reflections.

The apparatus must now be set up in front of the camera in such a way that the disc rotates in front of it, the hole passing the lens absolutely centrally once in each revolution. A tube of black card fixed to the lens, in the manner of a lens hood, and extending to very close to the disc, eliminates the danger of stray light entering the lens. The rotating disc functions as a kind of external shutter, giving regular short exposures.

The movement to be photographed must take place before a black background, and the subject must be well lit. The shutter on the camera remains open during the entire action.

The correct exposure is determined by experiment. If there seems to be too long a pause between successive exposures, another hole can be cut in the disc, directly opposite the first one, or the speed of the disc can be speeded up a little. By altering the gearing between motor and disc, it is also possible to slow down the rotation of the disc, should it be found that the individual exposures are too close to one another. Changing the disc speed affects the exposure, and this must be corrected by altering the lens aperture accordingly.

Copying

Photographic copying is essential where half-tone or line originals, of which no negative is available, are to be reproduced, either at the same size or on a different scale. It is a useful tool, for example, in enabling one to visualize a final layout at the correct scale. Virtually any kind of original can be copied, including paintings, manuscripts, engineering drawings, sketches, printed pages, and photographic or other prints in either line or half-tone.

The line copy

A contrasty film must be used for line reproductions, and this should be processed in a contrasty developer. High-contrast "line" films are ideal for this purpose, and a hydroquinone developer is suitable for high-contrast development. A good copy negative of a black-on-white original should have absolutely clear lines on a solid black base.

The half-tone copy

Normal medium-contrast film material should be used for the half-tone copy, to assure retention of the entire range of grey tones. For high-resolution fine-grain enlargements an ultra fine-grain film of a speed of around 12 to 20 ASA should be used. In the case of colour originals, where the colours have to be translated as faithfully as possible into grey tones, panchromatic negative material should be used.

Copying equipment

The basic requirements are a copying camera, an easel for the original and lighting equipment. The copying equipment can be arranged either horizontally or vertically. In either case the camera must be mounted sturdily—horizontally on a solid bench, or vertically on a strong and steady column. The camera position must be easily adjustable, the film plane remaining at all times exactly parallel with the easel. The lighting requirement is four lamps—two will do for originals of moderate size—these being mounted on arms, symmetrically to either side of the original.

The illumination

The two or four lamps used should all be of the same intensity—60- or 100-watt opal lamps being quite suitable. The lamps should be mounted symmetrically to either side of the original at such an angle that no reflections can be cast into the lens. This can be checked on the focusing screen or can be worked out from the angle of view of the lens and the angle subtended by a line from the edge of the reflector to the near edge of the copy. A very glossy and dark original might, however, pick up the reflection of the camera lens, or some other camera part, and this is best cured by placing before the camera a large black matt card, which has a hole in it just large enough for the lens to poke through.

The combination of film type, exposure and development method should be so co-ordinated as to yield a well graduated half-tone negative, with maximum overall detail, which will enlarge well. Correct exposure can be determined either with an exposure meter, or through one or two practical tests.

DARKROOM TECHNIQUES

Certain photographic phenomena which occur at the darkroom stage, and which under normal circumstances might be regarded as "faults", can be exploited deliberately for the purpose of achieving special effects. Among these are excessive grain, reticulation, solarization, and melted emulsion.

Coarse grain structure

Sometimes it is desirable for a photograph to have a coarse "sandy" grain structure. This can be achieved by using a very fast film, which is inherently coarse grained, and by enhancing the tendency to graininess by developing either in a print developer or in a film developer which has been warmed up to about 24°C (75°F). Special high-contrast "line" developers also lead to an exaggeration of grain, at the same time yielding very hard negatives. Under-exposure of the negative, and an accordingly longer development time—to around 30 or 40 minutes—also causes the grain structure to be enlarged. As these are all deviations from standard development methods, the correct exposure and development time must always be determined by previous experiment.

The result of copying a coarse-grained negative on document film

The degree of graininess is further exaggerated, of course, by the use of miniature film, which must be enlarged to a higher degree, or by the selective enlargement of a small section of a negative—for basically the same reason.

It is possible to produce a pure black-and-white effect in the nature of the ink sketch, where there are only black-and-white areas, the intermediate tones being represented by a greater or lesser density of silver grains. This is the way:

The original negative, which has been given special coarse-grain development, is enlarged on extra-hard blue-sensitive film. This film can be handled in the darkroom under an orange safelight, in the same way as bromide paper. This special film is then developed in print developer, fixed, washed and dried. The resulting positive transparency is then reversed to a negative by contact printing on high-contrast film. The final enlargement can be made in the manner of the line reproduction.

Reticulation

If a negative is processed or washed in a too-warm solution, reticulation of the emulsion may occur. Reticulation takes the form of a regular wrinkle-like pattern. It is really a physical disintegration of the emulsion layer, and it can lead to very effective results when applied to the right kind of subject matter.

An enlargement from a reticulated negative

Solarization

If normal exposure is drastically exceeded, solarization occurs. It is a form of reversal—a direct picture of the sun, for example, might well appear black in the positive print.

But this type of solarization is seldom referred to in general photography. What the normal photographer understands by "solarization" should really, more correctly, be referred to as "pseudo-solarization" or the "Sabattier effect". This type of partial reversal occurs if "unsafe" light is permitted to reach the film during development. Normally this is a serious fault, rendering the negative useless. But produced intentionally and under careful control, it can lead to very effective and interesting results.

About two-thirds of the way through normal development the film is briefly exposed to unsafe light. Development is then continued. The initially unexposed sections will now blacken, whereas further development in those sections which had already developed to a fair density will be comparatively retarded.

The reversal is generally of a partial nature but, with the careful timing of the process—and with suitable subjects, having dominant areas of light and dark and a clear-cut outline—complete reversal can also be achieved. In the latter case only an outline, in the nature of the line sketch, remains.

Melting the emulsion

Whole or partial melting of the emulsion can lead to interesting, and sometimes grotesque, distortions. It is effective in the production, for example, of photo-caricatures from portraits.

A negative intended for this process must neither be developed in a tanning developer (such as pyrocatechin), nor must a hardening fixer be used on it. After washing, the negative is hung up to dry in the normal manner, and that stage is awaited where there are no drops of water left on either side of the film, but where the emulsion is still evenly wet and swollen. When this stage is reached, the negative is warmed by holding it over an electric hotplate; glass plates can be carefully manipulated over a spirit burner or gas flame.

As the emulsion melts it becomes shiny. When this happens, it can be made to flow in the desired direction by carefully tilting and rotating the negative. As

Darkroom Techniques

A solarisation effect with the original photograph

Melting the emulsion can give most
peculiar effects

soon as the desired distortion is reached, the negative
should be cooled in a horizontal position. By repeating
this process with a number of small areas within the
negative, making the emulsion flow once to the left
and another time to the right, all kinds of grotesque
distortions can be attained. Before each new melting
stage the emulsion must first be thoroughly dried again.

Tone separation

In the tone separation technique, as the name suggests,
the continuous tonal range from black to white is
transformed into a limited number of distinct tonal
steps. The truly photographic character of the picture
disappears, and the print looks more like a poster. A
normal photograph can be treated in such a way, for
example, as to result in areas of only four distinct
tones—namely white, light grey, dark grey, and black.

The first step toward achieving this end is the
production of the separation negatives. This can be
done by making a contact positive transparency of the
negative on contrasty film, and then making the
separation negatives from this. Alternatively, the tone
separation negatives can also be prepared from a
positive paper print.

Whichever method is used, a highlight negative, a
medium tone negative and a dark tone negative are
called for. The exposure times for these three negatives
might generally be expected to be in the ratio of 1 : 2 : 4.
Each negative should be fully developed, to assure a
good density. In a fast-working developer or an extra-
hard paper developer the highlight negative should be

Darkroom Techniques

A portrait against a black background makes a suitable subject for tone separation

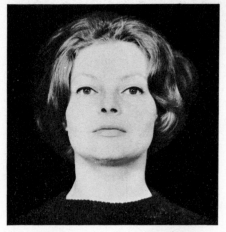

Separation negatives for a print with two tones

The tone-separated print has tones of black and grey only

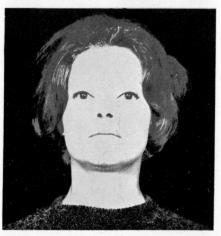

developed for at least two minutes, the two others being about three to four minutes.

The three separation negatives should look as follows:

1. Highlight negative: only the brighter highlights should reproduce a dense image on an otherwise clear negative.
2. Medium tone negative: All the medium tones, inclusive of the highlights, should reproduce as a dense image on an otherwise clear negative.
3. Dark tone negative: This negative shows all dark grey areas and all medium tones, including also the highlights, as a dense image, only those parts of the negative remaining clear which are to appear black in the final print.

All three negatives must be of extreme contrast. If it is discovered after development that there is still image detail visible where, in fact, the negative should be completely clear, this should be cleared with Farmer's reducer. Alternatively, the negative in question could be recopied once again, to eliminate the detail. This must again be done on extra-hard film, of course, producing first a positive transparency and from this the required negative.

To get the final print the three negatives are printed on one sheet of bromide paper, one after the other. The appropriate exposure for each negative can be determined in advance through the use of test strips. The highlight negative should leave the highlights a clear white, and should cover the rest of the paper with an absolutely even tone of light grey. The medium tone negative does not affect the highlights or the light tones, but superimposes its own darker tone of grey on top of the light grey in the appropriate places. The dark tone negative masks the entire picture area, with the exception of those parts of the print that are to be a solid black. The exposure given to this is such that the areas in question do, in fact, print to a solid black.

The tone separation process is also popularly known as "posterization".

Photograms

Using only an enlarger and sensitive paper—no camera being called for—it is possible to produce all kinds of photographic images. These are called "photograms". By laying an opaque object on a sheet of bromide paper on the enlarger easel and directing the light from the enlarger on to it, a negative type of silhouette outline of the object will be obtained. Upon development, the paper will remain white where the object was lying, and go black or grey everywhere else.

This simple method of producing photographic images without the use of a camera has many uses. By combining it with other photographic techniques, an unlimited variety of results can be achieved. Virtually any type or shape of article can be used provided, of course, that it is not too large. The shadow outline of the most irregularly shaped object can be rendered quite sharply by simply stopping the enlarger lens well down—this serving the purpose of making the illumination more directional.

Here are just a few possible examples:

1. An opaque plant or some other similar object is placed on a sheet of bromide paper, which is exposed through the well-stopped-down enlarger lens. The resultant print will show the object in negative fashion, white on a black background.

2. An object is placed on bromide paper, and moved during exposure, i.e. the light is switched on and half the exposure is given, after which the light is switched off and the object is moved to another position, the light being finally switched on again for the second exposure. In this way it is possible to produce photograms with different grey tones.

3. Transparent or translucent objects, such as glasses, bottles or thin materials can be used to make photograms in which a whole range of grey tones is retained.

4. A photogram can also be made on film material, which can then be contact printed or enlarged on bromide paper. This results in a black or grey object shape, on a predominantly white background.

5. Flat materials, such as pieces of cloth, leaves, screens of various shapes and patterns, and even crystals and very thin sections of fruit, and numerous other similar objects, can be placed on a sheet of glass in the negative carrier of the enlarger, and enlarged directly.

6. Unsharp or diffused outlines can be obtained by simply opening up the enlarger lens to its widest aperture, at the same time raising completely flat objects slightly above the bromide paper (with the aid of a sheet of glass, for example).

7. A simple small shape is cut from a large sheet of black card. The shape might be a circle, a triangle, a square,

Plant flattened under glass on bromide
paper and directly lit

Liqueur glasses laid on silver bromide
paper and directly lit

A turkey feather was laid on a sheet of film
and directly exposed. The print was
made from the resulting negative

Darkroom Techniques

A piece of laddered nylon stocking laid on photographic paper and exposed directly

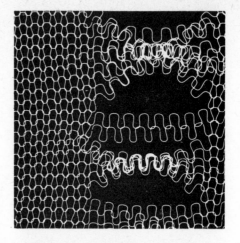

A piece of black paper with a hole in it was moved around a sheeet of bromide paper under the enlarger light

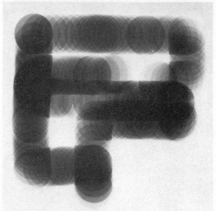

A document film negative with a circular clear spot was placed in the negative carrier of the enlarger. During the exposure, the enlarger head was moved up and down and the paper frame displaced simultaneously

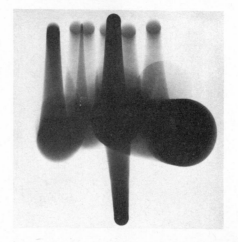

or anything else. The card is laid on a sheet of bromide paper, beneath the light from the enlarger. During exposure the card is moved about, sometimes slowly, sometimes faster, and sometimes it is permitted to remain in one position for a short, time. The light penetrates only through the cut-out shape, the black card shielding the remainder of the bromide paper. The resulting photogram consists of a complex pattern of partly blurs and partly sharp outlines, and a whole variety of grey tones.

8. A black-and-white ink sketch of any shape or pattern is copied on extra-hard film material. This negative is enlarged on a sheet of bromide in the normal manner— with the one exception that the enlarger head is carefully moved up and down on its column during the exposure. This will cause the outline of the original to be widened to a greater or lesser extent in its various parts, resulting in an interesting optical end-effect.

The examples given here should be regarded merely as suggestions. The scope is unlimited. Good photograms are very much the outcome of the will to experiment.

Although good photograms are sometimes created quite by accident, the consistently good results are produced by those workers who have a specific result, and a definite technique, in mind.

Adding a screen

While the principle of turning a conventional photograph into a half-tone reproduction is in no way complicated, it is generally not practicable to effect this transformation in the ordinary darkroom. It is best to ask a blockmaker to make a small half-tone negative from the print in question. A screen of between 85 and 133 lines per inch should be quite suitable. From such a negative, any number of enlargements can be made in the normal manner, using the normal enlarging equipment. The resultant photograph is a true half-tone picture, with large and small black dots, and is suitable for conversion into a block.

A similar effect can be easily created in the photographer's own darkroom, using finely gridded transparent film. But this will not produce a true half-tone effect: the dots will all be of the same size, but of different tones.

It is possible to buy sheets of transparent film printed

with screens of all types and sizes. Apart from dot and line screens, there are all kinds of irregularly grained and lined patterns.

To incorporate such a screen into the photographic enlargement, it must either be laid on top of the enlarging paper, or in contact with the negative. To get a really sharp image, the screen must in each case be in direct contact with the film or paper material. This is best achieved with a clean plate of glass.

It is possible to produce one's own screens by photographing such textures as sand, gravel, rice, wood grain, or sack-cloth. Some thin materials can be used as screens directly, without the need to photograph them. Among these are, for example, muslin, all kinds of netting material and very thin papers.

Pure black-and-white

The simplest type of graphic reproduction, the pure black-and-white (or "line") original, is generally also the simplest to print. An equally good result can be achieved on cheap newsprint as on an expensive art paper.

Virtually any subject can be converted photographically into a line illustration, often in just one stage. A great deal of tedious art-work can be saved in this way. The subject is photographed on extra-contrasty document copying film, which is then processed in an extra-hard working developer. This results in grain-free, two-dimensional negatives, having clear-cut outlines. If the required contrast is not achieved right away, the negative can be copied and recopied on

Against the light shot subsequently copied on document film to eliminate halftones

A normal photograph of a displaying peacock

The peacock photograph turned into a line drawing by the tone-line process

257

Low-sensitivity document film used
in the camera

extra-hard film, to yield the wanted black-and-white result. The contrasty copying films suitable for this purpose are generally of a very low sensitivity.

This method is particularly well suited to technical subjects, such as machine parts, tools, products of various types, and so on. The background should be either plain black or plain white, as is appropriate to the subject matter. If the subject is not to reproduce as a solid silhouette, but is to show some detail within its surface, it should be lit for distinct light and shadow areas. This is generally best achieved with an obliquely placed directional light source, such as the spotlight.

For such subjects as portraits and landscapes, the most suitable method for the production of line illustrations is that of the "bas-relief" effect, which is described below, and that of the exaggerated grain structure, which was discussed in the section on photographic tricks in the darkroom.

Bas-relief

It is possible to produce from a normal photographic negative a reproduction somewhat similar to an embossed image, without destroying the basic photographic character of the picture. This is done by the bas-relief method. In contrast with the more solid black-and-white print just discussed, and the black-and-white reproduction which relies on the greater or lesser density of its coarse grain structure for the effect of the middle tones, the bas-relief technique retains much of the fine detail of the original in the form of lines and relatively even grey tones. This process relies basically on the out-of-register masking of two identical images, one of which is negative and the other positive.

Any good negative, having crisp gradation and good sharp detail, can be used. The negatives should be at least of the format 2¼ in. square. If the wanted original negative is in the 35 mm. format, or smaller, this should be enlarged to a positive transparency which, in turn, should be contact printed to produce a negative.

The negative is placed in tight contact with a slow-speed sheet of film of good tonal gradation and, by exposing to the light of the enlarger, a positive mask is produced. This positive mask must have the same density and gradation as the negative. If the negative and the positive mask are placed on top of each other

Bas relief effect

in exact register, a completely uniform black surface should be the result. All light and shadow areas cancel each other out. A certain amount of experiment, both in exposure and development, is called for in the production of an entirely satisfactory mask. A shortened development time will produce softer results, while extended development time will lead to higher contrast.

The bas-relief effect is achieved by placing the negative and the positive mask in tight contact with each other, and very slightly out of register. Instead of giving a uniform black area overall, as is the case when they are placed in register, this gives clear outlines and some detail begins to reappear in the mid-tones. It only remains to print the two combined pieces of film in this manner.

A similar method can produce a very different effect. The negative and positive films are placed on top of each other in exact register, but backing side to backing side, and not emulsion to emulsion as before. A straight frontal view of the combination should, once again, show a uniform black surface. An oblique view at, say, 45 degrees, will show distinct outlines, however.

This combination is placed in a printing frame, on top of and in close contact with a sheet of high-contrast film. One light is placed in such a manner as to shine upon the frame at an angle of around 45 degrees. While exposing to this light, the printing frame is rotated through a full 360 degrees at least once, but preferably many times. The negative produced by this

The rotation method of exposure
1 Positive mask (emulsion up)
2 Negative mask (emulsion down)
3 Document film (emulsion up)
  Rotating base
4 Opal lamp or tilted enlarging head

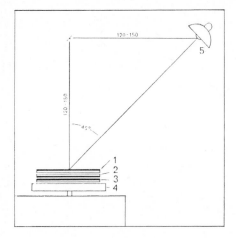

method is re-copied by contact on to another piece of high-contrast film. The result is a negative which will yield black line prints on a clean white base.

The rotation of the printing frame can be effected ideally by placing it in the centre of the turntable of a record player, from which the spindle has been removed. The player is set in motion, and the exposing light, at an angle of 45 degrees, is switched on for the required length of time.

The thickness of the lines in the final print can be increased, if so desired, by inserting a thin sheet of transparent material between negative and positive mask, to increase the spacing between them.

COMBINATION IMAGES

There is frequently a need for a type of picture which simply cannot be produced in the normal straight-forward photographic manner. This is where the combination of two separate images into the one picture can be called upon. Strictly speaking this type of montage is, of course, cheating—but it is perfectly permissible when the result justifies itself!

This kind of combination can be effected in two basic ways: by registering the two separate subjects on the same negative, or by combining the images on two different negatives in one final print.

Black background

The combination of two separate images on one negative is comparatively easy where an absolutely black background is used, as the only light to reach the film is that reflected by the subject matter itself. It is possible, for example, to take a close-up photograph of a transparent glass jar, and later to make a second exposure, this time of a person—again before a black background—carefully positioning the two images in relation to each other in such a way that, in the final print, the person appears to be inside the jar. To achieve this, the outline of the jar must be carefully

Photomontage against a black background. First a close-up shot was made of the spoon and glass and the crouching child was added by a second exposure

marked on the ground-glass screen of the camera, before this is moved for the second exposure, so that the person is sure to be positioned absolutely correctly. It must be emphasized again that the background must be absolutely black and non-reflective.

Background projection

It is frequently necessary to make a picture which is set in some distant or not easily accessible place. This kind of photograph can be shot in the studio, with the aid of background projection. All that is needed is a slide which contains the suitable background setting. One might even be able to find this within one's own collection. A suitable translucent projection screen is placed in the centre of the studio. The slide is projected on to this screen from the side opposite the camera position. The slide should be laterally reversed in the projector, so that the image appears the right way round from the other side of the screen. The subject should be placed on the camera side of the screen in such a way that the direct light beam from the projector is obstructed at the camera position.

At this stage we will just see a silhouette of our subject, against the projected scene. In lighting the subject great care must be taken to balance the intensity of the subject illumination with that of the comparatively weak screen image. The lighting must also be arranged in such a manner that no shadows are cast directly on to the screen. It is, furthermore, important to see that the lighting in the projected scene and that on the subject are consistent, i.e. if the sun is clearly shining from the left side into the screened scene, the main light of our subject must also come from the left.

Should the projected image prove to be so weak that any available form of lighting is too intense for it, then two separate exposures can be given—a long one for the screen image, while the subject is unlit, i.e. in silhouette, and a short one for the lit subject. It is of course essential that the subject remain completely static during this entire time.

If the subject which is to be placed in the artificially produced surroundings is small enough, a normal paper enlargement is often more practicable than a projected background image. But the projected image does have the distinct advantage of having a comparatively greater brightness range, and thus more

An Arab market scene with an empty
foreground

The figures in the foreground were cut
from another picture and pasted
into the composition

brilliance. It is also possible, of course, to produce a large positive transparency on film material, which is then illuminated from behind through a sheet of opal glass, or some similar translucent material—but this method has, of course, distinct size limitations.

The paper enlargement affords the operator a degree of control which is not possible with the projected image. He can, for example, print the enlargement as light or as dark as he wants, and he can also print it more or less contrasty. The enlargement must be illuminated absolutely evenly, and care must be taken that the subject itself casts no shadows on this background. (In those few cases where a shadow is deliberately wanted on the background, this is best done on a printed background, of course, and not a projected one.)

This type of image combination has many advantages, the main one being perhaps simplicity. It is really a case of making a normal photograph and a copy at one and the same time. By bending the lower part of the background enlargement forward, and placing the objects to be photographed on to this, the believability of the situation can be considerably further enhanced. In order that this bending of the enlargement does not lead to distortion in the final picture, it is essential that the bromide paper beneath the enlarger be bent up in precisely the same manner at the time the enlargement is made. By directing the camera perpendicularly at the background print, the distortion at the enlargement stage and the distortion at the re-photographing stage will cancel each other out, so that the foreground of the scene will look quite normal again.

Negative montage with masks

This image combination technique can be used to depict an object in a scene, in which it is actually not to be found. Let us assume that a model of a piece of modern sculpture, the original of which is not yet available, is to be shown in the location where the work is to be ultimately placed. It is not possible to move the model out to the location, and even less possible to transport the location into the studio.

First a correctly lit photograph of the model is made, before an entirely black background. Without moving either the model or the camera, the black background is changed for a white one. The lighting is then re-

For negative montage with masks, the sculpture was first photographed against a black background

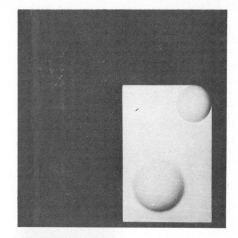

Stages in producing the negative montage. First, a document-film negative of the sculpture is converted to a positive by contact printing. The positive mask is printed together with a positive of an exhibition scene to provide a negative with a masked-out area to take the original photograph of the sculpture

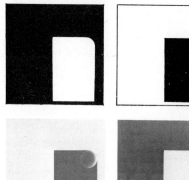

The masked negative and the original negative of the sculpture are printed together

265

arranged in such a way that only the background is illuminated, the model standing in complete silhouette. This second shot is made on extra-contrasty film material, and this is also developed for extreme contrast. This silhouette negative is reversed by contact to a positive transparency, showing the outline of the model in dense black, the entire background being absolutely clear. This positive "mask" is placed in the film carrier, in direct contact with the sheet of film upon which the scene is to be photographed. Thus nothing appears on the negative in that position where the sculpture is to stand. The negative of the model, which was made in the studio, is mounted in contact with the negative of the scene in such a way that the image of the model falls exactly in the empty space on the location negative. The two are enlarged together in this manner, to yield the final print of the sculpture in its future setting.

Negative montage with local reduction

This method is not suitable for cases such as the above, where two images must fit each other exactly, but it is useful in those cases where picture elements flow into each other with less precision. One advantage of this method is that it can be effected with existing negatives. (If the chosen negative is not to be destroyed, a copy negative should be made from it first—and this should be subjected to the reduction treatment.) It is equally possible, of course, to produce special negatives for this type of montage.

The first negative must be reduced with Farmer's reducer to complete transparency in those parts where image material from a second negative is to be introduced. The reduction should be done carefully with small wads of cotton wool, taking great care that those parts which are to remain intact are not affected. For contours, and for very small areas, the use of a fine brush is recommended.

On the second negative only those image parts which are to appear in the final picture are left intact, the entire remainder being reduced to complete transparency. Where there is image in one negative there is transparency in the other, and vice versa. When they are dry, the two negatives are bound together and enlarged simultaneously. It is not important if film negatives are not in exact emulsion-to-emulsion contact, so long as the enlarger lens is stopped fairly well down.

Artificial moonlight

It is possible to combine a negative of a scene with one bearing only the image of the moon, of snowfall or of rain, to introduce one or other of these phenomena into the final print artificially.

Here is the way in which a moon can be added to a picture of a scene which, at the time it was photographed, had no moon. On a clear moonlit night a negative is made of nothing more than the moon. (An exposure of around half a second at f 5·6 on medium-speed film should be about correct.) If one has a specific landscape shot in mind, the moon should be positioned on the film in such a way that it will occupy the correct place on the landscape negative, when these two are put together. If the moon negative

A normal shot by daylight suitable for conversion to a pseudo-moonlight shot

The overprinted daylight shot with a superimposed "moon"

is prepared on film, and not on a glass plate, it can later be laterally reversed for printing, if this is wanted.

A stock moon shot is best taken with a lens of fairly long focal length. It is also a good idea to use negative material somewhat larger than that one normally uses for one's landscape photography. The former gives one a larger moon image, and the latter makes it possible for the smaller negative of the scene to be moved around on the moon negative until the moon is in exactly the right position.

The scene to which the moon is to be added should be photographed at dusk. Alternatively, an under-exposed negative of a daylight scene will also do. The final print should, of course, be printed very darkly.

The moon negative should have a perfectly clear background. The two negatives are bound face to face and enlarged together.

Through infra-red photography it is possible to obtain a very realistic moonlight effect, even in bright sunlight, and this realism can be enhanced even further by printing in the actual moon image. Care must be taken to see that the shadows in the scene fall in a direction which is consistent with the position of the moon.

It is possible, of course, to shoot a scene with the moon in it directly on one negative, but this has two distinct disadvantages. Firstly, the long exposure time required by the scene would make the moon look like some sausage-shaped object rather than round, due to the movement of the moon through the sky during the exposure. Secondly, photographed in a normal scene, the moon looks much smaller than it appears to the eye in reality, so that such shots are generally rather disappointing.

Artificial snow

Let us now have a look at the way in which snowfall can be added to a scene. It is not always possible to wait for the desired fall of snow and, furthermore, it is not really desirable to expose the camera to such conditions. Again, a montage trick can save the day. And again it is a case of having one negative of the scene, and another of the snow. The snow negative can be prepared by artificial means, or by photographing a genuine snowfall. In the latter case, a black background is placed out in the open, and the snow falling in front of this is photographed. The background should, of

A normally-photographed winter scene

Artificial snow overprinted on the "straight" photograph

course, be as light-absorbent as possible, and the exposure time should be long enough to register the falling flakes as short streaks rather than points. The camera itself should be shielded from the snow. The background of the resultant negative should be quite clear, and even the image of the falling snow should not be too dense. One or more such negatives can be enlarged in conjunction with a negative of some appropriate winter scene.

Should one wish to depict a snowfall under quite calm conditions, where the flakes fall to the ground very slowly, this is best done at night, using electronic flash. This job can be done from the comfort of the home—the camera need only be pointed out of the window. It is a good idea to make several exposures on one negative, each one being set to a different distance.

If there is no real snowfall forthcoming, we can create its effect artificially. A piece of black velvet, or some similar material, is stretched over a flat piece of board and fastened to it. Sugar crystals or medium-sized crystals of cooking salt are spread evenly over this surface. The surface is then lit from a very oblique angle by the light of just one lamp—ideally a spotlight. The crystals will stand out brightly from the dark base. The camera is pointed straight down at this surface, and a time exposure is given, on fairly contrasty negative material. Care should be taken not to over-expose. During exposure the board is slowly moved in a straight line across the picture area. In this manner a quantity of blurred streaks are registered on the negative, in much the same way as happened with the real snowfall. Here again the final stage is the simultaneous enlargement of the negative of the winter scene and the snowfall negative. If the snow negative is too dense, it should be reduced to the correct level, as it would otherwise have an adverse effect on the final print quality.

Artificial rain

The technique for creating artificial rainfall is very similar to that used for artificial snow. The black velvet base must now be somewhat larger, and the salt or sugar crystals must be spread somewhat more sparsely. During exposure, the black base is given a long straight pull, to create the familiar continuous streaks of rainfall. To assure that these streaks will be straight, the black base should be pulled along some straight guiding edge, like a ruler or a straight strip of wood. To appear realistic, the rain image should not be too dense on the negative. The rain negative must, of course, be enlarged in conjunction with a scene where the ground is wet, and where the addition of rain is in every way appropriate.

An impression of rainy weather can be created very effectively by photographing the scene through a wet window pane. This, too, can be simulated. A vertically positioned plate of glass is placed in front of a boiling kettle. The steam will condense on the glass. When sufficient condensation has settled on the glass, the water will begin to run down the pane. At this point the kettle is removed and the sheet of glass is photographed.

One lamp lights the glass from the side against an

even black background. Care must be taken that no condensation settles on the camera lens. A little density in the background of this negative need not be harmful—on the contrary, this can soften contrast and help to create the feeling of greyness and sombreness of a rainy day.

Combination printing by stages

In each of the methods we have just described, the final enlargement can be made in one stage: the "main" negative and the "detail" negative are placed in the enlarger on top of each other, and enlarged as one. But this is possible only when the detail negative is on a completely transparent base, i.e. when it was shot against a black background. If the detail itself is dark, and is shot against a white background, this would give a negative of a dense background which, quite clearly, could not be enlarged simultaneously with any other negative—as it would completely obstruct the other image. Such negatives must be printed separately, one after the other, on the same sheet of paper. In such cases great care must be taken to assure that the second image is printed in exactly the correct position on the paper, in relationship with the first image.

This exact register of images is particularly important in the type of work described earlier under "ghost photography". As we have seen, a ghost photograph on a black background is easily made by photographing the two component parts of the picture on the same negative, against a black background. Unless the two separate parts of the whole picture happen to occupy

Phantom photographs on white backgrounds call for double printing from two separate negatives

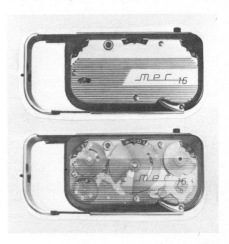

271

exactly the same relative positions in the picture area, this technique is not possible with the use of a white background. In this case two separate negatives must be made, and these must be enlarged—not simultaneously, but one after the other—on to one sheet of paper.

A combination print of the type described here can easily be made from two negatives of differing sizes. After having drawn an outline of the major part of the first image on a sheet of paper on the enlarger easel, this sheet is removed and replaced by a sheet of bromide paper, and an exposure is made. The exposed sheet is replaced safely in a box, and the first sheet of paper is replaced in exactly the same position on the easel as before, great care being taken also to assure that the easel itself is not moved to the slightest extent during the entire operation. The second negative is then placed in the enlarger, and enlarged to the desired size. It is positioned in the desired place in relation to the first image. The bromide paper which already contains the latent image of the first negative is then carefully replaced on the enlarger easel, and the second exposure is added. The end-result will be a "ghost" photograph on a white background.

LETTERING AND AIR BRUSHING

With a little skill it is quite possible to do good lettering with brush and paint directly on to a photograph. If a print is intended for blockmaking and extensive reproduction, however, or if several photographic prints are to carry lettering, it is best to copy the lettering photographically.

Black lettering

A preliminary enlargement of the photograph that is to bear the black lettering is made, to the ultimately required size. The lettering can be printed in the desired type and to the required size, or it can be drawn by an artist. It should be on high quality white paper, to assure the best results. A sheet of tracing paper is attached to the enlargement, and marks to indicate exact register are made in the corners of both enlargement and tracing paper. The line of lettering is cut out, and affixed to the tracing paper in the required position. Tracing paper, complete with lettering, is then removed from the enlargement, and copied on high contrast film, placing a sheet of white paper beneath the tracing paper, to assure a more solid background in the resultant negative. If there are any marks on the negative, showing where the lettering was stuck on, these can be removed by applying photo opaque to the negative at those points.

The original enlargement is placed on the enlarger easel, and the corresponding negative is put in the enlarger. The image is sized and placed so as to coincide exactly with the enlarged print. The scene can now be exposed on as many sheets of paper as necessary, these being replaced in a box immediately after exposure. They should be marked to indicate which is their top end and which the bottom. The negative is now taken out and replaced with the negative bearing the lettering. The original enlargement is replaced in its exact position in the enlarger easel, and the second negative is sized and placed in such a way that the registration marks coincide.

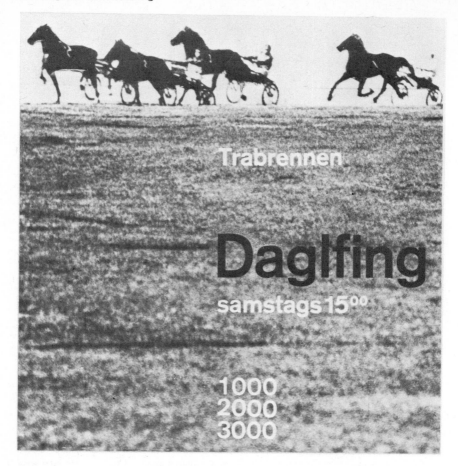

Print with black-and-white lettering
copied in

The exposed sheets of paper need now simply be returned to the easel, one by one, and exposed to the second negative. The end-result will be an enlargement complete with black lettering where it was required.

White lettering

The printing of white lettering into a photograph calls for an extra preparatory stage, but has the advantage that the two negatives can be enlarged simultaneously.

The first stage is once again a preliminary enlargement of the required photograph, this time the entire negative area being enlarged, regardless of the ultimate cropping requirements. Printed or painted lettering of the required size is cut out and attached to a tracing paper overlay as before, and the position of each of the corners of the print is marked exactly on the overlay in the form of a small cross. The overlay, complete with lettering, is photographed lying on a sheet of white paper, as before, but this time great care should be taken to assure that this negative is of the same size as the negative of the corresponding photograph. Any marks that may show where the lettering was attached to the overlay can be removed on the negative with photographic opaque. The resultant negative is contact copied on contrasty film to produce a positive, containing black lettering on an absolutely clear base. The negative of the photograph and the positive lettering transparency are enlarged simultaneously by mounting them on top of each other. The registration marks on the lettering transparency must be placed so as to coincide with the corners of the photograph negative. The ultimate combined enlargement can, of course, be cropped as desired.

Lettering with a screen

Both black and white lettering can have a screen introduced in printing it on to a photograph. In the first case, a piece of self-adhesive transparent foil bearing the required screen pattern is simply stuck to the negative of the lettering. In the case of white lettering, the screen material is also adhered to the lettering negative, before this is converted to a black on clear base positive.

The air brush

When purely photographic techniques or tricks fail to produce the exact effect that is desired for quantity reproduction by printing, the air brush can be called into play. With the air brush it is possible to emphasize the foreground, and to subdue the background, or to completely spray out the background to form a uniform surface. Although the spray applied by the air brush is entirely compatible with the nature of the photographic image, the matt colour coating upon the print which results is quite clearly visible. The truly photographic nature of the picture is, therefore, only regained in the ultimate print.

The air brush is a small paint spray gun, working with compressed air. The spray gun has a small paint container, and is connected to an air supply, such as a compressed-air bottle or a mechanical compressor. When a trigger is pulled, a fine tapered needle

Parts of the airbrush:
1 Needle valve
2 Trigger
3 Reservoir
4 Air tube

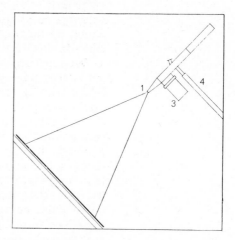

valve, which normally closes the jet at the tip, moves back and allows the air to rush through, taking the paint with it in a fine spray. The further the trigger is pulled, the more paint is released. Only limited pressure should be applied when spraying small areas from close up, but when larger areas are treated from a greater distance the pressure should be increased.

Only special air brush paints or high quality water colours should be used in the air brush. These have very finely ground pigments, which will not block the fine jet. A blocked jet is the worst thing that can happen during spraying: the jet suddenly spits little blobs of colour on to the print, ruining the entire work.

Air brush technique

For good and safe air brush work, the following important points should be remembered:

Always mix the paint in a clean pot, and do not attempt to use dried up paints, as they cannot normally be fully redissolved. Put the paint in a container with a close-fitting lid, to protect it from dust. Use a good brush for mixing the paint—not one which loses its hairs.

An ideal way of filling the air brush is to use some kind of pipette. Mix the exact colour that is required to a smooth consistency and, before spraying on the print, test the colour on a piece of paper. Remember that the colour will look lighter when it has dried. At the same time make a test to find the best spraying distance for even paint coverage.

When everything is right, start spraying the print. Spray evenly, stopping every now and again to check the depth of the tone that has been applied. Allow the paint to dry at regular intervals. Never spray continuously until the whole surface is running wet, as the paint will then tend to gather into puddles.

Masking

The outline sprayed by the air brush is, of course, diffuse. For sharp contours masks must be used. A wide variety of materials can be used for masking, including celluloid, transparent plastic film or even another bromide print. Transparent masks are generally more satisfactory than opaque ones, as the outlines of the picture can be seen through them.

Lay the transparent masking material on top of the print that is to be treated, and trace round the outline where the spraying is to take place with a sharp needle. The masking film can then generally be broken away quite easily along this engraved line.

A bromide print can be used as a mask in the following way. Make two identical enlargements, one on double weight paper, and the other on single weight. The single weight print is used as the mask, the required portion being simply cut out and applied to the other print. The mask, no matter of what kind, must be appiled firmly to the print so that the jet of the air brush cannot raise its edges, and permit paint to get underneath. The mask can simply be weighted down, but a more satisfactory method is to stick it down on the print with a rubber cement (e.g. Cow gum). When the paint is completely dry, the mask is pulled away again, and any remaining gum is cleaned off the print.

Special separation varnishes are also available. These are painted on to the print to mask out the required image area. After spraying is complete, the mask is easily removed by pressing adhesive tape on it. As the tape is removed, the mask comes off with it in the form of a thin film. These varnishes are particularly useful for masking fine detail, such as tree branches or complex frameworks.

A common error in masked air brush work is the application of too much paint. Frequently an almost imperceptible change of tone gives just the right effect. Before the mask is either lifted for checking purposes, or removed altogether, the paint should be completely dry.

In mixing the colour it is important to see that not only the tonal value is correct, but also that the colour characteristic of the paint corresponds to that of the grey in the photographic print. The unequal sensitivity to different colours of the photo-sensitive material used at the blockmaking stage can lead to unnatural looking results if any kind of colour cast is permitted to affect the photograph.

If the air brush work should be spoilt, the print need by no means be discarded. The paint is simply washed away again with water. Small mistakes, such as when the paint has penetrated below the edge of the mask, can be tidied up by removing the paint with a damp brush. Wipe away the paint, rinse out the brush, and repeat this operation as often as may be necessary. Fairly large areas can be cleaned up in the same kind of way. Damp the paint well with a large brush, and soak it up with a clean sheet of blotting paper. Repeat this process until the area becomes cleaner and cleaner, and eventually the last trace of paint has disappeared.

When the spraying work is finished, the final touches are added with brush and paint. The outlines are strengthened or tidied up where necessary, and those places where the mask might not have been cut quite correctly are touched in.

Extending the background

Frequently a picture that is required to fill a specific space is found to be not long enough in one direction. The print must thus be extended. If this is simply a matter of extending a uniform grey background, this is easily achieved with the air brush. If the print has a large enough white border of its own, the background can be extended on this through air brush paint-work. But the print paper is generally not large enough, and the extra background must be applied to a special transparent overlay. The print is first mounted on a sufficiently large sheet of card, or some other stiff base. The transparent overlay is fixed on top of this. The overlay must cover the entire print, and must extend to a sufficient extent on the side or sides which require the extra background. The air brush work is applied to the overlay in exactly the same way as to the print itself. The contours and details can later be finished off with brush and paint, where this is necessary.

INDEX